S0-BZU-619

Respecting Babies:
A New Look at Magda Gerber's RIE Approach

Ruth Anne Hammond

ZERO
TO
THREE®

National Center for Infants, Toddlers, and Families

Washington, DC

Published by

ZERO TO THREE
Toll-free orders (800) 899-4301
Web: www.zerotothree.org

The mission of the ZERO TO THREE Press is to publish authoritative research, practical resources, and new ideas for those who work with and care about infants, toddlers, and their families. Books are selected for publication by an independent Editorial Board.

The views contained in this book are those of the authors and do not necessarily reflect those of ZERO TO THREE: National Center for Infants, Toddlers and Families, Inc.

These materials are intended for education and training to help promote a high standard of care by professionals. Use of these materials is voluntary and their use does not confer any professional credentials or qualification to take any registration, certification, board or licensure examination, and neither confers nor infers competency to perform any related professional functions.

The user of these materials is solely responsible for compliance with all local, state or federal rules, regulations or licensing requirements. Despite efforts to ensure that these materials are consistent with acceptable practices, they are not intended to be used as a compliance guide and are not intended to supplant or to be used as a substitute for or in contravention of any applicable local, state or federal rules, regulations or licensing requirements. ZERO TO THREE expressly disclaims any liability arising from use of these materials in contravention of such rules, regulations or licensing requirements.

The views expressed in these materials represent the opinions of the respective authors. Publication of these materials does not constitute an endorsement by ZERO TO THREE of any view expressed herein, and ZERO TO THREE expressly disclaims any liability arising from any inaccuracy or misstatement.

Cover and text design and composition: K Art and Design, Inc.

Copyright © 2009 by ZERO TO THREE. All rights reserved.

For permission for academic photocopying (for course packets, study materials, etc.) by copy centers, educators, or university bookstores or libraries, of this and other ZERO TO THREE materials, please contact Copyright Clearance Center, 222 Rosewood Drive, Danvers, MA 01923; phone, (978) 750-8400; fax, (978) 750-4744; or visit its Web site at www.copyright.com.

10 9 8 7 6

ISBN 978-1-934019-35-1

Printed in the United States of America

Photo credits:
Julia Albee: cover, 6, 9, 11, 62, 69, 79, 81, 83, 108, 123,
Ruth Anne Hammond: 27, 42, 45, 48, 50, 57, 59, 65, 85, 91, 96, 99, 100, 107, 129

Suggested citation: Hammond, R. A. (2009). *Respecting babies: A new look at Magda Gerber's RIE approach.* Washington, DC: ZERO TO THREE.

*This book is dedicated
to my friend and teacher,
Magda Gerber;
to those who raised me,
Virginia, Gene, Annetta, Thelma & Irene;
to my partner in life,
John;
and to the best teachers of all, my children,
Marcus and Ivy.*

Their love and wisdom have made all the difference.

Table of Contents

Part I: Building Security and Creating Cooperation Through Respectful Interactions

Part II: Initiative, Integrity, and Autonomy

Foreword

I loved reading this book! It's a book I've been waiting years to hold in my hands—a complete, comprehensive explanation of Magda Gerber's RIE philosophy. I'm especially pleased because Ruth Anne focuses on both parenting and child care, tracing some of the roots for group care back to Dr. Emmi Pikler's research and the practice at the Pikler Institute in Budapest, Hungary. That sounds kind of heavy-duty, but this book isn't that way at all. It's wonderfully readable—full of information illustrated with stories, examples, and the author's personal experiences. As I read it I felt like I was sitting in a room with Magda Gerber as nuggets of wisdom poured from her lips. I also enjoyed new nuggets I had not heard before—Ruth Anne's own wisdom!

Magda was always bucking the tide of current trends, and if she were alive today she would be discouraged to see how parents are still stuck in the super-baby syndrome and infant care teachers feel pressure to get babies ready for school. Just one example is all the toys there are that have bells and whistles, do dazzling things, move, make noise, and attract attention. We think that babies have short attention spans, but that's because well-meaning people continually distract them with entertainment. As Ruth Anne says, "If stimulation is regularly of the 'entertainment' variety, the baby may become a habitually passive recipient who expects always to be entertained, rather than an active investigator." Without realizing it, parents and infant care teachers give babies the kind of entertainment that provides the perfect recipe for growing a couch potato, a video gamer, a seeker of entertainment rather than a seeker of knowledge.

I especially appreciated the way Ruth Anne sensitively worked in cultural differences and even pointed out some related to my European-American culture that struck a familiar note with me. I have always had the dilemma of wanting to teach people the particular philosophy that fits so well for me, but isn't culturally attuned to everybody. Ruth Anne handled that issue amazingly well.

While reading what Ruth Anne had to say about sharing I remembered a scene in the 1970s when I was an intern in Magda's Demonstration

Infant Program. I was sitting with three other interns watching two 15-month-olds struggle over a toy. This had gotten to be a pattern with these two children and, as always, the boy let go right away and the girl walked off with the toy. She was always taking things from him and he let her, though he looked disappointed every time. We wanted Magda to do something to make it fair! But she didn't. She just told us the two of them would work it out sooner or later. We didn't believe her, but several sessions later we did.

That particular morning started the same as the others. The boy got there first and was enjoying walking around with a small ball. The girl arrived and immediately grabbed it away from him. The boy looked upset. He walked over and picked up a small basket—immediately the girl took it. Then the boy picked up a plastic block—same thing! She grabbed it from him and put it in the basket. When she came for the puzzle piece he had in his hand, he held it out to her. Then he went over and got a purse and gave it to the girl. Then came a small blanket, but by now she was so overloaded she could hardly hold another thing. He was headed for a doll when she dumped all the toys in a pile on the floor and walked away. The game was over—and though she may not have learned to share at that point, she did stop taking things from the boy. Problem solved without any adult intervention. We interns were relieved, but Magda was matter of fact about it. "Children can solve their own problems," was her comment delivered with a shrug.

We don't have Magda here in person any more to show us how her philosophy works in the real world. But now we have Ruth Anne's book. I feel honored to have been asked to write the Foreword for it!

Janet Gonzalez-Mena
Fairfield, California

Acknowledgments

In the process of writing about my experiences with Magda Gerber and with the RIE approach, I have depended upon the encouragement and support of many. I would especially like to thank:

My husband, John Hammond, who writes (and reads) with an eye for clarity and simplicity, and gave me invaluable feedback though every step of the process. He has my gratitude as well as my heart.

My RIE colleagues, most especially Carol Pinto and Deborah Solomon, who read with RIE eyes and helped me clarify a number of points, and Janet Gonzalez-Mena for her words of confirmation. Their praise raised my spirits just when I was feeling most anxious.

My friend Jeffrey Cohen, professor of neurology at Dartmouth, who had never heard of RIE before I asked him to read the manuscript. He became an out-of-the-blue cheerleader as I was running for the finish line.

The children of Magda Gerber—Daisy Gerber, Bence Gerber, and Mayo Nagy. Their support has meant the world to me.

Julia Albee, who took many wonderful photos of my Wednesday RIE class over almost 2 years. I am so thankful that she gave her time and talent to enrich this book and illustrate the RIE approach.

My colleagues at Pacific Oaks, Jane Rosenberg, Cheri Oltz, Maria Estela Rodriguez, and Maria Moyer (among others), who have cheered me on and cut me some slack throughout this process.

All of the families who have contributed to my learning process. First and foremost, I thank my own family, including my co-parent, John, and my children, Marcus and Ivy, for providing my real life "laboratory." And I thank all of the parents, grandparents, and caregivers who have allowed me to share their joys and challenges throughout my years of teaching and told me to hurry up and finish the book so they could read it. Finally, I offer thanks to all the babies and toddlers who have let me into their world and filled me with joy and wonder.

The people of ZERO TO THREE. Emily Fenichel's up-front kindness and enthusiasm propelled me from Beyond. Jeree Pawl's editing could not have been done with more intelligence, grace, and sense of fun; I just wish I had more excuses to visit with her. Finally, I thank Michelle Martineau Green and Jennifer Moon Li for all the hard work of getting the book out there.

I needed all their help and feel so lucky to have had it.

Introduction

Resources for Infant Educarers, which is widely known simply by its acronym, RIE (pronounced "rye"), offers the tools with which to translate the idea of respect into action when caring for infants and toddlers. It is an integrated, multilayered approach that balances the need for freedom with the need for secure relationships. Relying on nonjudgmental observation to build understanding of the infant's needs and competencies—along with skilled, responsive caregiving—RIE practitioners aim to create mutually respectful, authentic, and cooperative relationships (Gerber, 2002). Why do some children enter school ready to learn academically and to thrive socially, whereas others do not? In addition, why do some parents enjoy their children and others seem to feel continually burdened and frustrated? The RIE approach provides answers to these questions and many others.

R IE was founded in 1978 as a nonprofit through which Magda Gerber could spread some very innovative ideas, based on respect for the child, about rearing infants and toddlers. The basic assumption of her RIE approach, and of this book, is that what adults do with infants and toddlers either supports or undermines their inner drive to learn and to develop their unique capacities as human beings. The RIE Approach is meant to provide the necessary scaffolding for infants and toddlers to maximize their capacity for self-regulation and purposeful activity, within the context of a few special relationships with parents or other deeply involved caregivers. The body of the book outlines the elements that, when applied as an integrated approach to child rearing, produce children who are joyful, authentic, competent, cooperative, motivated, self-regulating, and responsible. (See box Basic Principles of the RIE Approach for principles developed by Magda Gerber.)

Basic Principles of the RIE Approach

- Basic trust in the child to be an initiator, an explorer, and a self-learner
- An environment for the child that is physically safe, cognitively challenging, and emotionally nurturing
- Time for uninterrupted play
- Freedom to explore and interact with other infants
- Involvement of the child in all caregiving activities to allow the child to become an active participant rather than a passive recipient
- Sensitive observation of the child in order to understand her needs
- Consistency and clearly defined limits and expectations to develop discipline

Reprinted with permission from the Resources for Infant Educarers brochure.

From Hungary to Hollywood: The Evolution of RIE

After the devastation of World War II, Europe was filled with children whose parents were either dead or unable to care for them. To address this problem in Budapest, Hungary, the Hungarian government invited Magda's mentor, eminent local pediatrician Emmi Pikler, to create a model residential nursery. It would provide full-time, round-the-clock care for up to 40 such abandoned and traumatized children, ages birth to 3 years, avoiding the devastating "hospitalism" seen in other homes for orphans in Europe and elsewhere (Gerber & Johnson, 1998). Dr. Pikler continued providing pediatric care for local families, which was the context in which Magda, as a young mother, first met her. Magda was so impressed and startled by the respectful way in which Dr. Pikler spoke to and treated her ailing little daughter that she felt she must learn more.

In time, Magda began to apprentice with Dr. Pikler to learn her methods. She earned a master's degree in early childhood education and worked with Dr. Pikler at the National Methodological Institute for Infant Care and Education, usually called "Lóczy," after the name of the street on which it is located. The two women, who had once had daughters in kindergarten together, became more than teacher and apprentice; they became collaborators and friends. Their relationship spanned time and distance, lasting until Dr. Pikler's death in 1984, long after Magda and her family had left Hungary for the United States during the Hungarian Revolution in the 1950s. The institute is still in operation under the direction of Dr. Pikler's daughter, child psychologist Anna Tardos. It was renamed The Emmi Pikler National Methodological Institute for Residential Nurseries in Dr. Pikler's honor on its 40th year of operation (Tardos, 2007). (Throughout the book for the sake of brevity, I refer to it as The Pikler Institute or simply Lóczy.)The institute is still an important educational center for those who wish to learn and implement the Pikler approach around the globe.

After a short time on the East Coast, where Magda worked as a translator at Harvard University, Magda, her husband, and their three children relocated to Los Angeles. Magda took some time to become acquainted with "how it goes" in America, then reestablished herself as a therapist. She worked with children with cerebral palsy at Children's Hospital (her first order of business was to liberate them from their wheelchairs to allow them freedom to move as they could) and with children with autism at the Dubnoff School. Her success with these children, she claimed, was based on her respect for what they could do as opposed to expecting or pushing them to do what they could not. This is also where she started her first parent–infant classes with typically developing children. This was a bold innovation, and the jumping-off place for the evolution of Magda's genius in working with parents.

In time she began to collaborate with pediatric neurologist Tom Forrest of the Children's Health Council in Palo Alto, California. They codirected the Demonstration Infant Program in Palo Alto to apply Pikler's methods in families with typical, high-risk, and distressed infants.

In 1978 they founded the nonprofit Resources for Infant Educarers as a way of providing support and training for parents and professionals involved in the care and education of infants. The term *educarer* was conceived to express the integral concept that the education of infants is in the care they receive, and vice versa. Until after Magda's death in April 2007, the RIE Center was housed in the lower unit of her modest Silverlake duplex overlooking downtown Los Angeles. From this humble house on the outskirts of Hollywood, the message of respect for infants has spread almost stealthily across the United States and beyond, quietly attracting students and supporters from around the world.

My Long Road to RIE

The first time I was ever put in charge of a baby is one of my most vivid memories of childhood. I came from a rather small extended family, and I was the next to youngest of my in-town cousins, so we never had

babies at family gatherings. However, there was a baby who lived on our court of about six houses. One day another neighbor child and I were playing house on her front porch. We must have been 7 or 8 years old. Mrs. Revelle came across the street carrying her almost-1-year-old daughter, Two-Two (her nickname, having been born on the second of February). She asked us if we would keep her while she cleaned house to get ready for a party that night. We were thrilled. A real baby to play house with. How perfect! Mrs. Revelle went back to her house and we did what little mothers do—held and rocked the baby until she fell asleep. I thought I was in heaven to have that little warm head of dark curly hair resting on my shoulder. When Two-Two's mom came back to get her, however, she was not so happy with our successful caregiving. Her intention had been that we would keep the baby awake, so she would go to bed early before the party started, but she did not tell us that. So much for that plan.

It was another 26 years and two careers before I heard of Magda Gerber, but through my whole life I had always had a keen interest in babies and what they need. By the time I came into contact with Magda, I had migrated from Oklahoma to Texas, back to Oklahoma for high school, back to Texas for college, to New York as a professional dancer, then to Los Angeles to join my future husband, John. As fate would have it, we settled near Silverlake, and I eventually fulfilled my lifelong dream of marriage and motherhood. One rainy night my husband and I made our way to our prepared-childbirth class, which was to have a guest speaker. Elizabeth Memel, my current colleague on the RIE Board of Directors, came to talk about RIE. I was intrigued; it sounded interesting, if a little strange. The next day I drove the 7 minutes from my apartment up through the Silverlake hills to Magda's house on Murray Circle and bought *The RIE Manual for Parents and Professionals* (Gerber, 1979). It made so much sense to me that I got my husband to read it, too. By the time our son, Marcus, was born, we were ready to try it out. While I was recovering from a difficult C-section, John gave Marcus his first RIE diaper change, talking our newborn through every step. After a few months, even though we could little afford it, we enrolled in one of Magda's Parent–Infant Guidance classes. It felt like home—a wonderful place to just "be" with our child in a safe and supportive environment. It was the best, most peaceful 2 hours of our week. John and I both gained confidence as parents under Magda's mentorship.

Between my two children, who are 5 years apart, I started the training to become a RIE Associate. I was given the stamp of approval by Magda to teach RIE just before my daughter, Ivy's, class was to graduate, when the last toddler turned 2. The parents suggested I start a post-RIE group because I was certified, which I did. I rented space for the class from my church in Hollywood. (Not coincidentally, RIE is now housed in that same space since the disposition of Magda's home and the RIE Center on Murray Circle after her death.)

I enjoyed facilitating the toddler–parent group, but realized I needed more than a RIE certificate to feel really well qualified to guide parents. (I made some mistakes that make me cringe to remember.) Fortunately, the stars aligned and I was able to start earning my degree at Pacific Oaks College in Pasadena, where Magda had taught for so long. In 1996, I received a master's of arts degree in human development, with dual specializations in infant and toddler development and parent/community work.

As a graduate student, I was honored to be Magda's teaching assistant. After I received my MA, I was proud to be her coinstructor. After her retirement, I have continued teaching her signature course, Authentic Infant/Competent Child, among others. It still feels more than a bit presumptuous, but students continue to be inspired by Magda's teachings. I never tire of showing her videos and introducing others to the RIE approach and Emmi Pikler's work.

Since 1996 I have also been the master teacher in the Pacific Oaks Children's School Infant–Toddler/Parent Program in Pasadena, California, an appointment for which I must thank Renatta Cooper (for recommending me) and Yolanda Torres (for hiring me). Teaching at RIE and at Pacific Oaks has been my greatest learning experience since motherhood itself, and I am grateful for all of the families, more than 600, who have so graciously facilitated my growth.

At a recent RIE Conference (an annual event), I was asked by one of my colleagues in the RIE Alliance of Associates (open to those who have completed all three levels of RIE training) what would make this book different from other books about RIE. Feeling rather on the spot, I paused and said, "It will be different because...because...it will be written by me."

In 1980, Tom Robbins wrote, "The better the idea the more volatile it is. That's because only the better ideas turn into dogma." Because Magda was so eloquent, so wise and so beloved, it is tempting to try to freeze her teachings into some sort of template for perfection. However, this would not be in the spirit of her intentions. Her authenticity commanded our attention and admiration, but she never meant for us to do as she said simply because she said it. Magda meant for her students to find their own way of being authentic. This book is an attempt to communicate the wisdom I gained from being an apprentice and a friend of Magda Gerber, without compromising my own truth. This book describes how RIE has made itself known to me, how it fits with other things I have learned, and how I think it might be used by others who have the good fortune of working with infants, toddlers, and their families.

Parent–Infant Guidance Classes

The classes Magda started teaching in Carol Pinto's garage in 1973 were of her own invention, not derivative of any other person's work. Although there were several interim variations, the weekly classes settled into a format of bringing together a few (no more than seven or eight) parents and their similar-aged infants in a safe yet challenging environment for 1½ or 2 hours. In that time, parents were encouraged to quietly observe their children, watching to see what they were interested in and how they interacted with the other babies or toddlers while being available when needed, but not interjecting their own ideas into the children's play. Magda or a RIE intern would model selective intervention if conflicts between the children or safety issues came up. Toddlers were offered a structured snack experience (Magda always served bananas and watered apple juice). After an observation period of 20 minutes or thereabouts, parents were given the opportunity to tell what they had seen. Then they would have a chance to ask any questions that had come up for them in the week between classes. Magda would often open this part of the discussion with an open question: "So…how goes it?"

Those of us carrying on the tradition of RIE parent–infant classes try to stay as close to this model as we can, because it works. More about the various elements involved in such classes will be covered throughout the following chapters.

RIE Trainings

For many years, Magda traveled around the country and abroad, talking about how to demonstrate respect for infants. Many, many people come up to me now and speak fondly of her, thrilled to have had the chance to "sit at her feet" and learn about her approach. She spoke at National Association for the Education of Young Children and local conferences, consulted in child care programs, and created a small but effective system for empowering others to teach her approach—the RIE Certification process. The first step, RIE I, consists of a 2-week intensive or a 12-week evening course that covers theory and observation. She always used the RIE and Pikler videos, and had students go out and observe in RIE parent–infant classes and child care centers, reporting back what they had seen. The next step, RIE II, covers the practicum, in which the student interned in one or more of her parent–infant classes in order to learn to demonstrate the approach in groups of infants. The final stage, RIE III, offers the student the opportunity to practice communicating the approach by helping to teach RIE I courses. An important element in the certification of new RIE Associates [an official earned designation, therefore capitalized] has always been that the person be able to demonstrate the respectful values of the approach in all of her or his professional dealings with adults and children. A person was certified when Magda said she or he was ready.

Nowadays with Magda gone there is a somewhat more elaborate process whereby aspiring RIE trainees are mentored by several RIE Associates. It takes time; the approach must be internalized more than memorized. It is a process that should not be rushed. There are currently 40 RIE Associates actively teaching and consulting, and RIE parent–infant classes are offered in a number of U.S. cities and in Canada, with more in the works. RIE Associates are invited to teach in Europe, Asia, Latin America, Australia, and New Zealand. RIE is spreading its wings, and perhaps Magda is smiling somewhere, realizing that her wisdom still inspires.

References

Gerber, M. (Ed.). (1979). *The RIE manual for parents and professionals.* Los Angeles: Resources for Infant Educarers.

Gerber, M. (2002). *Dear parent: Caring for infants with respect* (expanded edition). Los Angeles: Resources for Infant Educarers.

Gerber, M., & Johnson, A. (1998). *Your self-confident baby: How to encourage your child's natural abilities—From the start.* New York: Wiley.

Robbins, T. (1980). *Still life with woodpecker.* New York: Bantam Books.

Tardos, A. (Ed.). (2007). *Bringing up and providing care for infants and toddlers in an institution.* Budapest, Hungary: Pikler-Lóczy.

Part I

Building Security and Creating Cooperation Through Respectful Interactions

Chapter 1

Touch With Care

The way we adults handle infants tells them so much about our attitude toward them. The gentleness or roughness with which we lift, carry, and manipulate their bodies determines how willing they are to open themselves to us, and to the world, because we represent their world in the beginning, and we are their primary link to the rest of it. How human culture is first conveyed to infants is quite literally in our hands. This chapter describes how one can make the daily events of infants' and toddlers' lives—such as diapering, feeding, bathing, or therapeutic interventions—opportunities to discover the joy of being alive and of being together with another person.

It was my privilege to attend the birth of my best friend's baby at a well-reputed hospital in the San Fernando Valley in 1996. It was a rather ideal, if medicalized, birth. My friend got the epidural at the first labor pain, and after 8 or 10 hours, she eventually pushed her daughter out with a minimum of discomfort. The baby was big, healthy, and very alert in the moments after entering her new—postuterine—world. As the nurse held her up, her father exclaimed at her beauty, and she immediately turned her head in his direction. She was ready, willing, and able to connect to her new world and its most important element, her people. Then she was taken to the nursery for her first bath. At her mother's request, I went with her. I was saddened to see that before she even had a name, she experienced her first assault.

What should have been a soothing and warm opportunity to connect with another person and become acquainted with her own body, this bath gave the baby every reason to withdraw from both. She was manipulated as though she were an inanimate object. She was scrubbed with a brush, turned, scrubbed some more, rinsed, and dried, more like someone was washing a dish than a brand new person. Understandably, her body posture was completely defensive; she rolled herself up in a ball and drew in her limbs in self-protection. As the gentle birth movement had been around for a decade or two, I had supposed neonatal nurses would show more sensitivity to newborns (Leboyer, 1975). I wondered if this was what my own two infants had been through in their early moments of life a few years earlier. I felt sad at that thought, and sad for my new goddaughter. I knew it did not have to be this way.

In a beautiful passage (excerpted in a 1994 *Sensory Awareness Foundation Bulletin*; Roche, 1994) in her first book, *Peaceful Babies–Contented Mothers*, Emmi Pikler wrote, "In the beginning, hands are everything for an infant" (p. 20). If the hands of the adult touch gently, move slowly, and take into account the baby's own movements and responses, the baby will not need to be defensive, and will open herself up to the other person and to the experience she is having. If the adult speaks quietly, describing what will happen, making requests and waiting for a response before proceeding, the infant will soon become a willing partner in the relationship and in the activities that constitute her care.

Dr. Pikler trained the caregivers, called "nurses," at The Pikler Institute to care for their charges in this way. To observe these nurses in action is a revelation. Even though they are responsible for their whole group of eight babies at any given time, they focus their attention on the infant being cared for, interrupting the care only when absolutely necessary, and with sincere apologies to the baby whose turn it is. It was Dr. Pikler's belief that if an infant has a warm, supportive relationship with one or a very few adults who attend very closely to the child during care activities, the infant will be sufficiently supported to be able to pursue productive and pleasurable independent activity during times when the other infants in the group are being attended to by the nurse. Her theory has proved to be a successful means of assuring secure attachment patterns in institutionalized children.

Each group of infants, usually eight, is cared for by a team of four nurses who take turns in shifts around the clock. One nurse is present at any given time, supported by an assistant who does not handle the infants but performs tasks such as bringing food, cleaning up messes, and delivering clean laundry. Each nurse on a team develops a "preferred" relationship with a small number of the infants so that each infant has one special person with whom to attach. This is the nurse who usually gives the daily bath, which is a special time between the adult and child, and writes the daily summaries for the child.

Anyone who performs any kind of bodily care for an infant—whether a nurse, doctor, child care provider, occupational therapist, family member, or teenage babysitter from down the block—can contribute to an infant's well-being by being mindful of the type of touch being offered. There are implicit memories being created in infants that will influence for life how they feel about themselves and their bodies, as well as what is reasonable to expect from others. They will not necessarily remember the specifics of how they were handled, but they will carry the memories in what they assume about themselves and the world without even being aware, until much later (if ever) that these assumptions are based upon concrete and repeated, but unrecollected, experiences in early life (Schore, 2003; Siegel, 1999).

Gentle, respectful touch translates into a point of view that says "I am a valuable person who has a right to be respected by others. Other people make me feel good; I like them." Rough, unmindful touch translates to "People can do with me as they please. My body isn't important. I need other people, but that doesn't make me comfortable. I must not deserve careful attention from others." The paradigm developed by an infant who has been truly abused or neglected would be even worse. Because people attract experiences that reinforce their basic assumptions about themselves, and resist those that do not, it is worth taking the extra few moments to make care routines and other bodily interventions respectful. A baby's future depends on it. An infant who has been physically respected by those performing intimate care is unlikely to become an adult who allows her- or himself to be roughly handled or habitually disrespected by others.

What does respectful care look like? What does disrespectful or unmindful care look like in a natural setting? It is easier to find examples of the latter than the former? How often does one see an adult wipe a child's nose without warning, or at least sufficient warning to allow the child to comprehend what's happening and participate cooperatively? As a teacher in a parent participation program, I frequently see adults walk up behind children and pull their wet T-shirts off, momentarily arresting their forward movement, forcing their hands up and blinding them as the shirt comes over the head. Would we ever do this to an adult? Of course not, but perfectly nice people do it to toddlers all the time, until they stop to think about it. These are examples of unmindful bodily care.

Continual repetition of these negative types of interactions starting from birth will have a subtle yet profound effect on a child's sense of self—that they are not in charge of their own bodies. By the time they are 3 years old, the traditional age at which preschool used to start, children should have at least the beginnings of clear boundaries as to what is and is not acceptable in what liberties others may take with their bodies. The best way to help them develop that knowledge is to teach them, through thoughtful and gentle handling during care or other interventions on their behalf, what respect feels like, right from the very beginning.

Even with something as simple as picking up an infant, enlisting the baby's cooperation is validating for the child, and makes the job easier and more enjoyable for the adult. It is surprising to see an infant barely a few weeks old cooperate by preparing her muscles for a change in altitude and position, when given the chance. Also, it is something anyone can do, no matter what his or her role in the child's life. Respect is conveyed in taking time to speak to the child ("I want to pick you up now, so we can get your bath started."), holding out the hands as a nonverbal cue, and waiting until the baby makes that slight muscular adjustment of cooperation before picking her up. It seems a little thing, but in the many repetitions of such moments, an infant learns that she participates as a partner with others.

If the adult has acquired the skill of picking up the baby in such a way as to interfere as little as possible with the baby's sense of bodily integrity and cohesion, so much the better. (See box Picking Up a Baby.) Making sure that the baby is able to maintain his equilibrium while being picked up takes only awareness and a little practice. The way this can be accomplished is to make a practice of picking up the baby in the same way all of the time so that the baby can anticipate what is happening. It may sound a little studied and unspontaneous, but a little technique adds to the confidence of the adult and is most helpful to the infant, who already has such a big job, to adjust to and learn about the world.

The bath is a wonderful opportunity to build on the relationship between adult and child, as well as to help the infant learn to tune in to his own body and the sensations coming through it into his awareness. As adults attune to the young infant in order to engage in the care of his body, we help him to develop many kinds of awareness. First is his bodily sense of self, or as Daniel Stern (1985) has named this awareness, the sense of the core self. The bath, as choreographed by Dr. Pikler for the children at Lóczy, supports first the awareness of the various parts of the body when the nurse wipes, with a cotton ball and oil, each crease in progression from head to feet. Then, as the nurse washes the baby all over with a soapy bath mitt, the infant feels his body as a whole. After soap is applied, the baby is placed in the water of the bathtub, and gently rinsed. The baby is invited to splash and enjoy the sensation of being in the water, and the nurse enjoys seeing the baby learn to create pleasure through his own bodily actions and senses.

Picking Up a Baby

Here is one very good way to pick up a baby, which I learned watching the nurses at The Pikler Institute. Practice on a baby doll until you feel smooth in the motions, then try it on the baby.

As you approach the baby, who is lying on her back, hold out your hands as you would to pick her up. Pause, making sure your face is the right distance from hers so that she can focus on you, and tell her you want to pick her up and why. If she is busy with a plaything, tell her you would like her to put it down, or give it to you, because it is time to do something together. Wait until she is ready to disengage from the object of her attention, then proceed slowly. (If the baby is on her tummy as you approach, let her know what you are doing, turn her onto her back and then proceed as follows. Always lifting her in the same way builds security.)

Lift her right shoulder slightly with your right hand. Slide your left hand under her head, replace your left hand under her head with your right hand, and slide your left hand along her spine to her bottom. At this point, she is securely in your arms, with her spine and head fully supported, her face at a good focusing distance from your own. Rise up and, if necessary, bring the baby's right arm forward, so it is not stuck underneath your left arm. Throughout this process, the baby has been able to see your face, and to keep herself "together" without any unnecessary jostling. Her integrity has been maintained as well as her attention to you.

To put the baby down, first lower her bottom onto the surface upon which you are laying her, then very slowly lower the rest of her body, supporting the head still with the right hand until the left hand joins the right. The head is finally, and very gently, lowered and released. With your face still fairly close to hers, let her know what will happen next, before you proceed with a task or move away. The idea is to avoid any abrupt changes because her ability to process change is much slower than ours. Slow transitions allow her to be able to "stay with" whatever is happening, rather than lose focus or tune out altogether.

It may seem like slowing down all of these moments of transition will make for an endless day. However, when the math is done, there is actually a net gain because by encouraging the infant to stay focused, adults are able to accomplish tasks more easily. A baby who is not in defensive reaction to the chaos of abrupt changes in location or stimuli is more willing to cooperate. Anyway, even if one is picking up the baby 30 times a day, adding 10 or 20 seconds to that action only adds up to an extra 5 to 10 minutes a day, which can easily be recouped through cooperation instead of upset and resistance during caregiving.

The bath also supports the infant's sense of connection to the adult, as the adult speaks to the infant not only about what the adult wants to do next ("I need to clean under your chin; can you lift it a little?"), but also about what the infant seems to be noticing ("Oh, you've put the corner of the towel in your mouth. Does it feel good on your gums?"). As the adult waits for the infant to move, spontaneously or deliberately, into a position that makes wiping under the chin easier to accomplish, the infant learns that her participation is desired and appreciated, which makes the experience more rewarding for both. (Tardos & Appell, 1992) Even if there is less than total cooperation, the adult acknowledges the infant's agenda ("Well, you are too busy chewing to lift your chin...but I've managed to clean your neck anyway. Now I'll wipe under this arm.").

A peaceful and pleasant bath, or any other important care event in an infant's day, might happen occasionally by chance, but it will be more likely to happen regularly, becoming the expected norm, if certain preconditions are rigorously met (Tényi, 2006). The elements that allow such focused attention during a care routine are listed below. Each element is addressed in detail throughout the chapter.

- The infant is in a quiet–alert state.

- The adult speaks to the infant quietly about what is happening and waits for a response.

- The adult is able to give the infant full attention.

- The adult has preset all of the needed equipment.

- The adult does not feel rushed.

- The adult has acquired some skill in how to handle a freely moving baby.

- The adult sees the relationship as more important than the task.

The Infant Is in a Quiet–Alert State

The infant is neither too sleepy nor agitated from fatigue, overstimulation, or hunger (unless the task is feeding, of course). If the baby is in a more active or agitated state to begin with, the adult can often gain the child's quiet attention by speaking sensitively about the baby's present state and surroundings, as well as about what the adult needs to do to help the baby now.

The quiet–alert state—with its characteristic wide-open eyes, steady heart and breathing rate, and readiness to pay attention—is the state of consciousness in which infants are most likely to learn. According to brain researchers such as Allan Schore (2003) and Bruce Perry (2004), the most important learning that infants have to do takes place in the context of relationships with others, and care routines are rich with important learning opportunities. The infant will learn about his own body; he will learn about what feels good and what does not; he will learn that his actions have meaning, and that he can elicit responses in adults. He will also be gaining language as the adult speaks about everything that is happening during the interaction. The template for give-and-take conversation, as well as other cognitive building blocks, is formed during these repeated routines.

The Adult Speaks to the Infant Quietly About What Is Happening and Waits for a Response

When an adult speaks quietly about what is happening and waits for a response, the child does not need to be on alert that a change could be coming at any moment unannounced. It is enough for a baby to have to regulate her emotions when unavoidable surprises happen, such as when someone accidentally drops something, making a loud noise. The adult should not expect her to stay in any kind of equilibrium if he or she swoops in, picks her up from behind, carries her off to the changing table and starts undressing her without giving her a chance to adjust to the idea.

Imagine you are slicing carrots for the dinner salad and someone comes up behind you, grabs your arm and, without speaking, drags you to the car to take you out to dinner. As you arrive at the restaurant, your companion notices you are still clutching the knife and reaches to take it out of your hand. Would you give it up gracefully? Would that be a set up for an enjoyable evening? Of course not. It is easier to enjoy something for which one has been prepared. Common courtesy dictates that people have a right to know what will be expected of them throughout the day, especially if some of it will not be of their choosing. Of course, infants do not hold a clock in their heads quite as well as older people, but getting into the habit of offering courtesy to an infant sets the tone of adults' relationships with them, which will make it more rewarding for the baby and for the adults.

Waiting a few moments for a baby to finish with a particular experiment with a toy and turning his or her attention to the adult's agenda is simply common courtesy.

The Adult Is Able to Give the Infant Full Attention

The adult does not feel pressure to split his or her attention between the child being cared for and other responsibilities. If those responsibilities include other infants or children, the environment is arranged so that the others are safe and also secure in their expectation that they will have a special turn with the adult as well. (More about arranging the environment is discussed in chapter 3.) This is a key component of the success of the RIE and Pikler way of being with children.

If you happen to be a therapist, or have ever been in therapy, you will know that one of the aspects of the experience for the client is the feeling of having the therapist's complete and undivided attention. The phone is turned off, there is a Do Not Disturb sign on the door, and only an event like an earthquake would interrupt the client's 50 minutes of the therapist's time. The therapy progresses well because of the quality of attention the therapist pays to the client. The first indicator of high-quality attention is that it is undivided.

This is exactly the same with an infant; infants become comfortable and secure on the basis of the quality of attention received from their significant adults. Anyone who has hands-on interactions with infants is, by definition, significant in their development. In fact, if a person has a weekly or biweekly session with an infant, it is even more important to assure the quality of the attention. There are not that many chances to make up for an unpleasant or unrewarding interaction on such a schedule. If a mother rushes or is distracted sometimes during a diaper change or a bath, there are many more chances for her to do it better the next time. If she is usually slow, gentle, and attentive, an occasional lapse is emotionally manageable for the child, and may even be helpful in the process of learning that her parent is human.

According to Stern (1985), an infant develops his expectation of what it is like to be in relationship with specific people in averages. Stern called them "RIGs," or "representations of interactions which have been generalized." Bruce Perry called them templates (Perry & Szalavitz, 2006). No matter what they are called, the more often an interaction happens, the more incidents get added together to create the averaged internalized expectation. (See box, Graduating From RIE?, for information on verbal cuing in interactions.)

If an infant experiences a visit to the doctor's office as a place where virtual strangers manipulate him; talk over and past him; and poke, prod, and even hurt him without explaining what they need to do or why, then that is what he responds to and comes to expect. Such an expectation

Graduating From RIE?

Infant–adult pairs who share many, many repetitions of interactions may eventually comfortably let go of the need for verbal cuing because their understanding of one another is so deep and the nonverbal is more than enough for both to feel a sense of cooperation and communion. However, this sort of understanding usually emerges only in people who intimately live together, so it is safer for professionals who work with infants and young children to assume that the inclusion of language to scaffold a caregiving activity is useful to the child. Here is a true story to illustrate just how long it can take, even in families, for the verbal cues to become superfluous.

> A fastidious mother reported that she was helping clean her 4-year-old daughter's bottom after a messy poop on the toilet. The mother, as always, gave the child a warning before using a wet wipe. "Here comes the wet wipe. It's going to be cold." The child had been hearing this since she was a newborn infant, but only on this day did she finally say, in exasperation, "Mommy, you don't have to say that. Do you think by now I don't know the wipe will be cold!!??"

does not make it easier on the child, the parent, or the medical personnel at the next visit. On the other hand, if the infant is included in the conversation, and if the doctor or other practitioner calmly explains what she must do and what is needed from the child in cooperation, the child comes to see the doctor's office as a place he may not like to go, but at least he learns that he can know what to expect and feel at least genuinely regarded as a person. A lollipop after a disrespectful examination or procedure does not erase its negative emotional consequences. A focused, empathetic, and thoughtful interaction, even if it involves something unpleasant to the child, will support the child's self-respect, and allow the child to learn to trust and respect others.

Whether it is 10 diaper changes a day, six meals, a daily bath, a weekly occupational therapy session, or a monthly doctor visit, infants will benefit from the presiding adult's thoughtful and undivided attention. This is an important aspect of an infant's education, because how adults pay attention to infants scaffolds their ability to pay attention throughout life. The multitasking that the world has come to expect of adults is not good for babies.

The Adult Has Preset All of the Needed Equipment

Everything is conveniently at hand for the task so that there will be no interruptions during the interaction. If the baby is playing on the floor of the child care center and you notice she needs a diaper change, before picking her up it makes sense to take a few minutes to make sure there are no children in your group now needing more immediate attention, the changing table is not already in use, there are diapers and plenty of wipes in the diaper cubby, and her clean clothes are near at hand. This sort of prechecking should become an ingrained routine that you do automatically. Even if the baby is crying, it is better to let her stay with his discomfort while you prepare the bottle or the food, rather than holding her insecurely with one arm while clumsily opening the baby food jar with the other.

Infants can learn patience by having their needs met in this calm and collected way. One of the best pieces of advice Magda gave me as a new mother was to go ahead and take the time to go to the bathroom to make myself comfortable when the baby woke up hungry at 2:00 a.m. She said he would learn to trust me if I told him, "I'll be there in one minute, sweetheart," and that he and I would have a more peaceful feeding if I did not start it on the toilet. This scenario illustrates perfectly the principle that proper preparation, even if it means the baby has to wait a couple of minutes, enhances the relationship.

The Adult Does Not Feel Rushed

See the previous section on presetting all of the equipment. Use the toilet first. Also realize that rushing does not actually save time, but it keeps the baby from paying attention. The issue of our attitude toward time and how it impacts attention span is more fully discussed in chapter 9. Suffice it to say here that if the RIE approach had only two words of guidance to get its point across, they would be "slow down," especially during bodily care. Care is not something that is seen as an interruption of the adult's or the baby's activities, but as an important opportunity to be together.

To maximize the learning opportunity and relationship-building prospects of an interaction, it might be worth delaying a diaper change or other intervention for a little while, until a fussy baby is more able to participate fully. If there is no way to allow for a delay, then at the very least the adult can still provide a model of calm compassion as the care proceeds, acknowledging that the baby would rather not. Speeding up to "get it over with" when the baby is crying usually backfires; it only further

agitates her. Proceeding in a peaceful and gentle manner is more soothin
even if it takes a few more minutes.

When the baby's attention wavers from the necessary task to pursue
another line of investigation (i.e., play), the adult is willing to share the
child's attention. The adult allows time to appreciate what the child finds
interesting before gently guiding the child's attention back to the task.
This give and take of personal agendas sets a positive tone for the overall
relationship and for the infant's sense of self.

The Adult Has Acquired Some Skill in How to Handle a Freely Moving Baby

When infants become very mobile, it is in their nature to move. It is in
our (caregivers') nature to want them to be still and let us do what we
have to do, like they did before they could flip over in an instant. If we
are willing to adjust our expectations at this point and allow infants to
"call the shots" with regard to their own position, we are showing them
that we respect their needs. And if we respect their needs, we can reasonably expect them to respect ours. It has long been my belief that the
reason people feel that 2-year-olds are "terrible" is that a 2-year-old has
the capacity to protest when he or she feels disrespected, and that takes
adults by surprise. It is my contention that if adults habitually respect
infants' developmentally expectable preferences whenever they possibly
can, infants will not feel the sense of violation that leads to "terrible"
behavior.

For specific instructions on how to give a bath, The Pikler Institute has
produced a very useful training video called *Bathing the Baby: Concern,
Empathy and Acquired Gestures* (Vámos & Csatári, 2002). The premise of
the video is that if the adult learns the "how to" very well, then the quality
of the interaction will be improved because the adult will not have to be
consciously thinking about physical logistics and will be more available to
respond to the actions of the baby and the emotional events that unfold
during the care.

It is possible to learn how to adjust to infants' and toddlers' autonomy
of movement during caregiving routines. (Freedom of movement in general
is discussed at length in chapter 6.) This means if the baby wants to turn
over onto his tummy during a diaper change or bath, the adult will have
to figure out how to proceed with the baby in this position. Once a baby
is able to pull up to standing, he will usually choose to stand through diaper changes and dressing. With a little practice, adults find that it is easier
to gain cooperation from toddlers when they respect their choice of posi-

tion, rather than wrestling them into a position they do not like. One practical hint is that a vertically installed towel bar in a designated changing area offers a place for the child to hold on to for balance. With this little aid, the baby or toddler can help in changing even a very messy diaper by lifting one leg and then another as the adult cleans the child.

The Adult Sees the Relationship as More Important Than the Task

The adult is interested in learning what interests the child, and is willing to take the time to share the child's focus of attention before drawing her back to the task. Distraction is not used to manipulate the child's attention so that a task can be accomplished more quickly outside of the child's awareness.

When an adult has to do something that involves inflicting pain, there may be a role for distraction, but that does not mean surprising the child. Instead, being honest about what you need to do, while making distractions available for the child to use at will, is more respectful. A little boy in one of my parent–toddler classes was diagnosed near his second birthday with juvenile-onset diabetes. In the course of the next year, it was an honor to observe the respectful manner in which the boy, his mother, and his nanny handled the frequent pricks for blood testing and injections of medication that were necessary. By always telling him what they needed to do, by giving him a choice about where he wanted the prick (which finger?) or injection (right buttock or left?), they allowed him to maintain his sense of integrity, of owning his own body, so to speak. His emotional integrity was also supported in the way they allowed him to cry if he needed to without being cajoled or made to feel that his self-expression was unwelcome.

Over time, he adjusted to these intrusive, but essential, moments of care with equanimity, crying less frequently, and, oftentimes, choosing to distract himself from the pain by playing with something near at hand or talking about something else that interested him. A distraction is a good tool in lessening pain in such instances, but the distraction should be of the recipient's choosing and should not be imposed in lieu of honest communication about what is happening or going to happen. To be able to facilitate the child's self-control, the adults need to be aware of their own feelings. Of course no one likes to have to do anything that hurts a child, and there are many feelings awakened in adults by the crying of a child. Honesty is, however, the best policy, if the adults' priority is the child's basic integrity and earning her trust (Thomas & Edwards, 1995).

A disturbing experience I once had at my doctor's office is a gr
illustration of what the consequences of distraction during intimate
can be. I was there for my well-woman checkup. As the doctor wa:
my annual examination, she was talking to me about her upcoming
tion to Italy, about which she was very excited. When she finished, and
said, "OK, you're done." I had no idea whether she had examined my
breasts for lumps. (She said she had, when I asked.) I was appalled that I
had allowed myself to be touched without even paying attention to what
was being done to me. I was angry at the doctor for being so self-
absorbed that it seemed my health was less important than her vacation.
Giving her the benefit of the doubt, I suspect doctors often want to allevi-
ate a patient's embarrassment, or their own, through such distraction.
Mainly, though, I was shocked at how easily I was coerced into losing my
connection with my own body. I immediately thought about babies and
diaper changes, and how often they are distracted as their genitals are
being cared for. I am all for singing with babies, but if I am singing
Twinkle, Twinkle, Little Star to a baby as I am cleaning his penis, I am
turning his attention away from what he should be paying attention to,
his own bodily sensations. Should a baby be taught to tune out while
being touched? What might this be teaching?

A person who has responsibility for any sort of bodily care of a child
needs to work through her or his own discomfort or embarrassment concerning issues of modesty and messes. It is important for adults to accept
that infants and toddlers need proper, nonjudgmental language for all of
their body parts and products, including their genitals. It is normal for
infants and toddlers to touch as many of their own body parts as they can
reach. If adults do not override their internal valuing mechanism (Rogers,
1967) through distraction ("Here, play with this while I change you.") or
negative judgments ("Ooh, stinky!"), they allow children to learn how to
tune in to their own bodies in a way that will promote healthy self-esteem
and self-care.

Of course, they must test us. One of the points of pride at The Pikler
Institute is that the children tease their nurses during care routines
because this means that secure attachment has been attained. (Children in
substandard orphanages do not display this playful testing behavior with
the staff.) It is well known that children save their most challenging
"tests" for whomever they are most comfortable and spend the most time
with. In my work with families, and in my own family, I have seen this to
be true. Mothers often have a more difficult time getting a toddler on task
for a diaper change than does the child's caregiver. According to Ute
Strube (personal communication, February 11, 2006), the nurses at The
Pikler Institute are more challenged in this way when they have their own

children than with their Pikler babies. I found that to be more than comforting.

When an intervention simply has to happen now and the child is still not ready to consent, a good dose of active listening (Rogers, 1967) sometimes has to fill in the gaps where perfect cooperation is not happening. Again, a parent has many opportunities to redeem him- or herself, and (thank you, Donald Winnicott) only needs to be "good enough," not perfect (Winnicott, 1971). How "good" is good enough, of course, is always the question, and how this concept translates from parents to professionals is another. If high standards are valued, and practiced as a general rule, then normal deviations will be less onerous than deviations from lower standards.

When a child has had several notices that an intervention needs to take place but she still does not want to come, respectfully acknowledging this point of view and offering a couple of real choices will get past the resistance without damaging the relationship. Saying something like, "I know you want to keep playing. That is a fun dollhouse, but I have to change you now so you don't get a rash. Do you want to walk to the bathroom, or shall I carry you?" is a much better alternative than demanding and judging, "Get over here right now! Why do you always have to be so uncooperative? Why can't you be a good girl?" or just unceremoniously picking her up and carrying her off, screaming, to the bathroom. Of course, often she will not just drop everything and comply with one of the two acceptable (to you) choices, but, again, saying, "I guess you can't choose right now, so I'll choose for you. I'm going to pick you up now" conveys respect to the child without abandoning authority or responsibility on the adult's part.

The basic RIE principles (Gerber, 1979) of sensitive caregiving to keep in mind as professional standards are to (a) treat the infant as an active participant rather than a passive recipient of care; (b) follow and share the infant's focus of attention when it wavers from the task at hand and gently lead him back to the task; (c) allow the infant freedom to choose his own bodily positions during care; and (d) overall, slow down and use the task to invest in the relationship.

The next time you perform any sort of intervention—whether it is a diaper change or a physical examination, take three deep breaths before you start—observe the child for a few moments to assess her state of consciousness, and only then proceed, with the intention of working with the child as your partner, to accomplish your goal.

References

Gerber, M. (Ed.). (1979). *The RIE manual for parents and professionals* (Rev. ed.). Los Angeles: Resources for Infant Educarers.

Leboyer, F. (1975). *Birth without violence.* New York: Knopf.

Perry, B. (2004). *Understanding traumatized and maltreated children: The core concepts.* (CD-ROM Educator's Package: Series 1) Houston, TX: ChildTrauma Academy.

Perry, B., & Szalavitz, M. (2006). *The boy who was raised as a dog and other stories from a child psychiatrist's notebook.* New York: Basic Books.

Roche, M. A. (Ed.). (1994). Emmi Pikler: 1902–1984. [Special issue]. *Sensory Awareness Foundation Bulletin, 14.*

Rogers, C. R. (1967). *Person to person: The art of being human.* Lafayette, CA: Real People Press.

Schore, A. N. (2003). *Affect regulation and repair of the self.* New York: W.W. Norton & Co.

Siegel, D. (1999). *The developing mind.* New York: Guilford Press.

Stern, D. N. (1985). *The interpersonal world of the infant: A view from psychoanalysis and developmental psychology.* New York: Basic Books.

Tardos, A., & Appell, G. (1992). *Paying attention to each other: Infant and adult during the bath* [DVD]. Budapest, Hungary: The Emmi Pikler Institute.

Tényi, V. (Ed.). (2006). *Bathing the baby: The art of care.* Budapest, Hungary: Pikler–Lóczy Társaság.

Thomas, G., & Edwards, W. S. (1995). *Making the patient your partner: Communications skills for doctors and other caregivers.* Westport, CT: Auburn House.

Vámos, J., & Csatári, I. (2002). *Bathing the baby: Concern, empathy and acquired gestures* [video]. Budapest, Hungary: Pikler–Lóczy Association for Young Children.

Winnicott, D. W. (1971). *Playing and reality.* New York: Methuen.

Chapter 2

'Round the Clock Routines

When a baby can count on the rhythm of his day, life is easier for him, and for the adults who care for him. A child who falls into easily recognizable wake/feed/play/sleep patterns may "train" his caregiver from a very early age to create a daily routine that helps him to anticipate what will come next, which builds a sense of security. A child who displays less natural regularity may need even more carefully adhered to sequencing of daily events to help him create a sense of inner order, although this may take extra patience. Magda Gerber's mantra was that infants thrive on what adults consider "boring sameness." In this chapter, I discuss the meaning to the infant of routines, and how to use the elements of the daily events to maximize healthy development.

When adults hear the word *routine* they usually think of something to be tolerated but not particularly enjoyed. They think of a "routine checkup" at the doctor's office, or "same old routine" at work. The *Oxford American Dictionary & Thesaurus* (1996) defines routine as "a regular course or procedure, an unvarying performance of certain acts...a set sequence in a dance, comedy act, etc." I suggest that for infants, the second listing is more accurate than the first when it comes to caregiving moments.

While being fed, diapered, or bathed, the young infant is, metaphorically, in rehearsal for the dance of life. Caregiving is not performed in an "unvarying" manner either. It is actually more like partner dancing, in which both members of the dance team need to know the steps, someone has to know the "leads," or cues, and someone has to read the "leads" in order to know which step of the dance is coming next.

In dancing and in care situations, the more times the routine is rehearsed, the more secure in the steps and the more open to nuanced embellishments the partners become. A wonderful visual aid to see how this interactive "dance routine" looks when skillfully choreographed but creatively improvised is the video from The Pikler Institute called *Paying Attention to Each Other: Infant and Adult During the Bath* (Tardos & Appell, 1992). It shows a series of baths given by different nurses to different infants, and eloquently illustrates the quality of care described in the previous chapter, but with one not-so-great interaction included to show the difference between good communication and missed opportunities.

Lives are lived on a continuum with "unfaltering routine repetition" on one end and "total chaos" on the other. Most people would not want to live at either end of this continuum. Everyone's body must have certain kinds of care on a regular basis—like food and sleep—yet most people's innate drive to seek novel experiences keeps them from getting completely in a rut. Different people have different needs when it comes to balancing routine and novelty. Some people like routine and find it comforting, whereas others need more novelty, and sometimes find routine to be oppressive. Whatever one's own temperament, it is important for children's sake to find a balance between novelty and routine, because in spite of all their sensation- and novelty-seeking impulses, they also need the regularity of on-time meals, bedtime rituals that conform to their sleep needs, and the security of knowing what to expect, in general, from their days and nights.

The link between routine and self-discipline was the topic of an advanced workshop given for RIE Associates by Anna Tardos, the director of The Pikler Institute. She said that the first requirement for disciplining toddlers is the trust between the adult and child that grows out of sensitive caregiving on a routine basis (Tardos, 1996). So, a predictable life, with expectable routines, sets up an infant to become a child who is more easily able to display self-discipline and more willing to accept adults' guidance because he has developed trust in us. (Would you accept "guidance" from a person you have no reason to trust?)

Physiologically, keeping an infant's life predictable, with needs being met in a timely manner—meaning "on time"—by someone she knows really cares about her, allows her to internalize a rhythm to the day that provides her digestive system, sleep cycles, and nervous system the opportunity to get into a groove. Psychologically, this allows her to develop basic trust and security (Erikson, 1950). If meals, dry diapers, and rest are provided in a sequence that matches the infant's hunger, elimination, sleepiness patterns, the baby will be able to relax and not worry too r__ about getting her needs met. This is basic trust in the outside world to be a safe and friendly place. Security means assuming that hunger is quickly followed by satiety.

Some infants seem to already have a rhythm from just a few weeks of age; they are usually sleepy at the same times of day, hungry at regular intervals, and ready to play at somewhat the same time every day. Others display less regularity, and adults have to work harder to figure out how to structure a day that works for everyone (Chess & Thomas, 1987). Again, the metaphor of the partner dance works; the baby and the adult must be willing to see where the other will lead. If my baby is always sleepy at around 9:30 a.m., I should let him lead me not to sign up for a 10:00 a.m. class. On the other hand, if the baby is never sleepy at the same time, I might need to restructure a number of elements of the day so that maybe I can lead him to learn that 7:00 p.m. is pretty much always bedtime.

It is a difficult truth for many in our novelty-seeking society, myself included, but babies need predictability and regularity in their lives more than they need excitement and stimulation. (There will be more on this in chapter 9.) Adults should make the most adjustments rather than expecting infants to adjust to their personal or institutional convenience. Yes, babies are flexible and are designed to adapt to fit into the society in which they are born, but a society must embrace that meeting infants' needs is part of its function. It is a fact that the natural, slow-paced rhythm of the day in which human beings evolved as hunter–gatherers bears little resemblance to the fast-paced world people live in today. However, their biological needs have not changed since then (Perry, 2004). The greatest message Magda Gerber offered those responsible for infants is that they must make the effort to adjust to the infant's pace. There may be opportunities for fun and excitement that will be missed, but by letting go of that faster pace, they will allow the baby to learn and grow peacefully and at the tempo that supports her ability to stay in tune with herself and what is around her. I think of this as the foundation of holistic, or organismic, integrity.

I was once interviewed for an article in a pregnancy fitness magazine about how to fit the baby into one's life. The editor really wanted me to say that after 6 months of age, a certain number of car trips per day were ideal; I was to choose the number. When I said, "As few as possible," I was asked, "Well, how many is a few?" Ultimately, I refused to give a number, but reiterated the principle that riding in cars is useless time for infants, and should be considered as a necessary evil. Is the trip in the baby's interest? Will it lead to an event with meaning to the baby, such as a visit with Grandma or a chance to play with other babies? Or not? Of course errands must be run, but careful parents make arrangements not to impose them on their babies and toddlers any more than absolutely necessary. Just being in the same space does not constitute real togetherness.

Imagine you are getting together with a dear friend you have not seen in a long time. When you arrive at her house, she says, "Come on, get in the car; I have to run errands. We can catch up while I make my rounds," versus, "Come in; I'm so happy we have some time to spend together. Make yourself comfortable while I get the cake." Which will feel more like quality time? Chances are, the latter will make you feel more highly regarded, as well as more relaxed and at peace.

Magda called this kind of quality time "wants nothing time" (Gerber, 1979) because there is nothing on the adult's agenda but being together and seeing where the child leads. It is essential for infants to receive this kind of quality attention routinely. For one thing, this form of togetherness lets them know they are worthy of our undivided attention; for another, we learn to slow down and really see who they are and what they like to do. Another benefit is that it allows adults to feel we are meeting their need for us, even though we cannot give them our undivided attention all of the time. Perhaps they would like to have it all the time, but that is not a realistic wish. However, if we give some undivided attention every day while the baby/toddler/child is rested and ready to lead, he will not mind so much when we need him to play independently while we do what must be done. If he must go on errands or to pick up older children from school, at least he will have had some of our undivided attention, keeping in mind that trips into the community are more meaningful when the infant is included in the conversation with the drycleaner or grocer.

The other kind of quality time Magda (1979) talked about is "wants something time," when the adult has an agenda and needs to get something accomplished that concerns the child, like bathing, dressing, or feeding. Because these activities are routine, it is easy to slough them off as boring or unimportant, and just get them over with as quickly as possible. Treating care routines as quality time is a concept that has spread throughout the United States so effectively that now it is an explicit facet of all accredited infant care program standards (Copple & Bredekamp, 2009). This approach originally came through Magda, from her work with Emmi Pikler in Budapest, Hungary. Relationships are soundly built on a foundation of repeated daily care routines that engage the infant and adult in mutual communication and cooperation. From a RIE perspective, it is sad that parents so often have to, or even choose to, give over this important part of their relationship to others. The value placed on the care, including the quality of touch, communication, and pleasure, is transmitted directly, if unconsciously, to the child and contributes materially to her sense of value as a person. How could it not?

If an infant is allowed to stay home in the early postnatal weeks and is carefully observed by the parents, the infant will show them what his natural rhythms are for eating, sleeping, and playing. If he is taken out and incorporated into the adult's agenda right away, he will not have the chance to lead the way to a mutually beneficial routine. This attention to the infant's natural rhythms is espoused not only by Pikler and RIE, but also by T. B. Brazelton (1992). In his book *Working and Caring*, Brazelton was very clear that the widespread social policy in the United States of giving a mere 6 weeks of parental leave after the birth or adoption of a child does not offer adequate time. It takes longer for infant and adult to learn about each other so as to create mutuality in the family routine and optimal balance. He suggested that it requires a minimum of 4 months just to work out the nursing relationship. I think Brazelton would agree that even more time would be better in giving parents the feeling that they have all the time they need to get to know their baby's rhythms.

Until the United States, as a society, decides to support infants by allowing parents more time before they must return to work and all its stressors, it falls to the child care community, formal and informal, to create relationships and routines that feel natural to the child. Individualizing the care by way of thorough intake interviews with the family, plus detailed observation of an infant's cues, is the first step to establishing a routine that supports the infant's emergent self-regulation. Some questions to ask in developing the infant's individualized routine are as follows:

1. How do you know when she is sleepy?

2. How does she most often fall asleep in the daytime? At night?

3. What time(s) does she sleep in the daytime and at night, and for how long?

4. How does she wake up?

5. What usually happens first when she wakes up?

6. When does she like to play?

7. How long does she like to play?

8. Is she happy to play on her own?

9. For how long will she play on her own?

10. How do you know when she is getting tired?

11. What do you do when she is tired of playing?

12. How does she let you know she is hungry?

13. How often does she eat?

14. How much does she eat at different times of day?

15. How do you know when she is full?

16. Does she let you know when she needs changing? If so, how?

17. Does she like to be held?

18. How long does she like to be held?

19. How do you know she would like to be held?

As you can see from this list, there are a lot of signals that must be accurately read in attending to an infant. A person who is feeling rushed or stressed will probably not be able to focus his attention fully to "read the lead" a baby can give to help adults meet her needs. "Wait" is another meta-message from Magda that gives adults permission to delay doing something in order to observe to see if their assumptions may be wrong. Although prompt attention to an infant's distress is very important, it is not necessary to act before taking the time to make mental notes to tailor the response accurately. There is a saying in my family when we are spinning our wheels: "Do something, even if it's wrong!" However, Magda taught me it is better to wait than to jump in and do the wrong thing. Adults may not always do the "right" thing even after they have waited, but at least they are giving themselves the chance to consider alternatives.

So, a comfortable pace is needed to start building beneficial routines. These routines afford infants plenty of uninterrupted time to move through the cycles of hunger, sleep, wakefulness, and play, as well as to ensure adults adequate time for observation to learn the baby's cues, to see what the baby can do on his own, and become familiar with what he likes, dislikes, or ignores. Finally, the routines allow for feeding, bathing, diapering, and other caregiving opportunities to be quality times that enhance adults' relationship with the baby as well as the baby's sense of self.

An infant's ideal routine, then, is made up of a rhythmic ebb and flow of expenditure of energy (play and exploration in an interesting environment alone or with others) and opportunities for refueling (healthy food, sound sleep, and richly satisfying communication with the caregiving adult). Another memorable point Magda often made, which I learned was borrowed from our wonderful Pacific Oaks colleague, Elizabeth Jones, that relates to this topic is "the curriculum is what happens." This ebb and flow, whether at home or in child care, provides the optimal baseline level of stimulation an infant needs. Once the necessity of an individualized routine is acknowledged, maximizing the benefit of all the elements of the routine is the adults' challenge, including coordinating the child's routine needs with their own.

The topic of play and exploration, which according to RIE principles should be supported 100% of the time a baby is not asleep or involved in caregiving, is discussed in another chapter. How to use occasions of bodily care to maximize cognitive and social–emotional development has already been discussed in chapter 1. Discussion of sleep and feeding rounds out the topic of daily routines.

Sleep

Sleep is the single most discussed topic in all of my parent–infant/toddler classes for all of the years I have been teaching. It also took up lots of discussion time in my classes as a parent with Magda. Common sense and scientific research regarding sleep agree that good habits gained early have a healthy impact on the rest of life. Finding ways to help settle the youngest babies and helping older babies find their own ways to self-soothe are the fodder of folk wisdom as well as multiple bookstore titles.

The reason, with all of this attention, that sleep still causes such buzz among today's parents is that modern life and babies' biology are frequently at odds (Gonzalez-Mena & Widmeyer Eyer, 2008; Small, 1998). Adults are trying to fit a square peg in a round hole. They want to have it all: an exciting, full modern lifestyle and babies that sleep when they want them to. (That is one nasty joke of which parents are the butt.) The old adage that "everything costs" is true in this case, too. By not making sufficient adjustments to the biorhythms of babies during the day, adults pay at night when infants are overtired, overstimulated, and need too much help settling down. A very calm and regular daytime routine begets a nighttime routine that is also more predictable, less stressful, and more restful for children and adults alike.

In RIE-based infant programs, naps are always individualized. Children are not all expected to sleep at the same time or for the same amount of time. However, as Weissbluth (1999) suggests, it may be true that common biological sleep times exist so once a routine is established for a group, they may well fall into patterns of sleeping at the same time. According to Weissbluth, daytime sleep should occur at least two times during day: around 9 a.m. (1–2 hours), 1 p.m. (1–2 hours), and for the youngest ones a third nap around 4 p.m. (30–45 minutes).

How babies learn to fall asleep can help or hinder as well. When a baby is used to nursing to sleep, co-sleeping, or being rocked until asleep, she may have a more difficult time adjusting to the expectation when she begins child care that she will fall asleep independently. Extra patience is required of the caregivers and the parents. Working together to find solutions that will support the infant both at home and in care may be tricky, and fraught with emotion, but is essential. One of Magda's key suggestions was to put the child down to sleep before he or she is overtired. People tend to wait, thinking it will be easier, but this is a myth; being overtired makes it more difficult, not easier, to fall and stay asleep.

It is often not possible to replicate the family routines in child care, so it is necessary to help a baby adjust in as compassionate a way as possible, but without overdoing the empathy. Trusting that a baby is capable of a certain amount of independence if he has a chance to learn is more helpful than just feeling sorry for the baby and getting frantic to stop him from crying.

Crying is not the enemy. Lack of skill in self-regulating is. The adult's job is not so much about stopping the crying or "putting" the baby to sleep, but helping her find a way to let go of the outside world and enter the interior world of sleep. Making big changes the first week in child care may set up an unnecessary roadblock to trust. Trying to change a baby's habits before she has developed an attachment with her new caregivers will undermine both the establishment of attachment and of a workable routine. It makes much more sense to avoid a major shock to the child's expectations, and to slowly make incremental steps toward the acceptance of the culture of child care, in which children must be more independent than they are expected to be at home.

If parents know they will soon be placing their new babies in child care, allowing the infants to develop the skill of self-calming early on will make the transition to child care much easier for all involved. On the other hand, having to leave one's baby in the care of another all day makes those nighttime hours together all the more precious. Sensitivity regarding this issue on the part of the caregivers will go a long way in helping working parents feel understood.

With older toddlers, it is the regularity and activity of the daily schedule and the clarity with which nap times are valued by the educarers that promote the napping of all or most of the children at the same time, even the ones who resist naps at home. In the child care program for 2- to 3-year-olds at Pacific Oaks Children's School, the primary care groupings are called "nap groups," because a long time ago the teaching staff realized that the vulnerability of tired children at the transition to sleep warrants the attention of a special person to ease them toward sleep. A great deal of attachment is accomplished through the rituals leading toward sleep. Instead of building in work breaks just as children may need extra support, these teachers recognize that their calm and supportive presence will help the children find their way to sleep, with a few pats on the back, an extra trip to the potty, or that special favorite book being read one more time.

Knowledge of many children over time, and perhaps their own very real need for a little rest, makes clear to child care providers that napping is vitally important for the children and the program. Parents often have less experience on which to base their approach to sleep than child care teachers, and that can make it more difficult for them to set the stage for their children's sleep.

Clarifying values is usually a good place to start when working with parents on this issue. There can never be a one-size-fits-all answer to the question of how to get the baby to sleep at the right time and for the right duration because every family has differing variables to contribute and every infant has slightly different ways of responding to his inner and outer environment. Is it more important for the baby to fall asleep independently so that he can learn to put himself to sleep because all of the adults in the house really need a full night's sleep before the next day's work? Or is it more important for the baby to feel the comfort of falling asleep in closeness with a parent even if it means a parent will be awakened several times during the night to help the baby resettle? These are very personal family issues, and I never feel it is my place to make the call when there is a conflict between core family values and "best practices" kind of advice.

On a recent beautiful summer evening at an outdoor music concert in downtown Los Angeles, I was reminded of this rock-and-a-hard-place dilemma facing young parents. They want to expose their children to the delights of life, and there are many in the city, but in summer especially, this happens after children's normal bedtime. Is it worth disrupting established sleep patterns to hear some Latin jazz? I understand exposure to different kinds of rhythms in the first year of life is very beneficial to infants' later musical intelligence, so maybe it is. However, when disruptions occur too frequently, or a regular bedtime ritual is never really established, it is not surprising that parents find their little ones difficult to manage at night. Even if disruptions occasionally occur, it is easier for children who have established patterned sleep habits to return to those patterns, often with a sense of relief.

More than special occasions, it is the daily events that more often than not have a disruptive effect on the establishment of regular sleep patterns in infants. Perhaps the parents have irregular work schedules and the child stays later at child care on some days than others. Perhaps the grandmother, who is the caregiver, has to pick up the older sibling from school right at the baby's nap time, and when the mother gets home from work at 7:30 p.m., she needs time with the baby even though the baby normally would go to sleep at 7:00 p.m. Or maybe the mother is a night owl and just does not quite notice that it is too late for the baby to be up.

The point is that most people do not live in a time or place where life shuts down at sunset, or where everyone can take an afternoon nap to make up for the times the baby woke up at night. People's lifestyle and biology are at odds. Adults use electricity, caffeine, and other substances to help them through the day, but they want babies to do it naturally. Of course, many new parents are ready and happy to make the changes raising a family inspires, and lucky are their children.

The messages that Magda offered about sleep is that it is a wonderful privilege and babies are lucky to get to go to sleep whenever they are tired. She always recommended putting them in their beds just as soon as the very first sign of tiredness occurred, when they rubbed their eyes or yawned once. If a baby still could not go to sleep easily, the next night put her to bed even earlier. This is the method used at The Pikler Institute, and the infants there seem to put themselves to sleep peacefully. Each baby is given a soft "lovey" cloth for use in self-soothing, and finger and thumb-sucking is seen as healthy. (I have observed children there giving each other their soft cloths for comfort.) Sleep is highly revered, and it is a given that a tired baby should be in bed.

It has been my experience that it is this sort of clarity that promotes acceptance, by the baby, of the adults' values. When parents get very, very clear in their own minds about what they need to do to solve a problem on their children's behalf, the children fairly quickly get on board, whether it is about weaning, bedtime, or whining.

Magda helped me as a new mother to see the value of creating a sleep-time ritual that would be calming to my baby and help him to let go of the waking world, to know that it would still be there when he awoke, and to transition peacefully to the world of sleep. My husband and I used *Goodnight Moon* by Margaret Wise Brown (1947) to provide structure in our son's nighttime routine. When the book ended, we said goodnight to all of the toys and pictures and furniture in his little half of a room. Of course, in all honesty, the difficult part started when I put him in his crib and walked away. He did not want to let go of the comfort of a parent just because he was going to sleep. My ambiguity kicked in when he cried out. It was fueled by dueling values and beliefs, based on my exposure to multiple sources of advice to parents, such as William Sears's (1985) book, *Nighttime Parenting*, which espoused cosleeping, and the opposite, Richard Ferber's (1985) *Solve Your Child's Sleep Problems*. Ferber (2006), it is gratifying to note, has recently recanted his earlier blanket negative evaluations of cosleeping (Coukell, 2006). My family and I found our own way, on the basis of sometimes conflicting values and tolerance for sleep deprivation.

In working with families who are trying to transition out of "the family bed" and into more segregated family sleeping arrangements, I often quote sleep clinician Klaus Minde, from Montreal, Canada, who spoke at the ZERO TO THREE National Training Institute in 2000. He said he always tells parents who are at their wits' end with the difficulties surrounding their child's sleep patterns that even though their child may cry and protest, making the necessary changes in bedtime routines does not undermine the basic trust that their child has in them. It may feel horrible to listen to a crying baby or young child, but it is truly in the child's best interest to learn a way of sleeping that creates peace in the family, and the child will not lose faith in the parents if the parents are attentive and sensitive as a general rule all day and truly have the child's best interests at heart. The other thing he said at that conference that I have never forgotten is that if one studies the sleep patterns of families who come to his clinic for help and families that do not consider sleep to be a problem issue, the patterns are basically the same. It is the discomfort of the parents that define the problem. Meredith Small (1998) says the same basic thing in *Our Babies, Ourselves*, as does Janet Gonzalez-Mena in *Diversity in Early Care and Education: Honoring Differences* (2008).

That is why, as an interventionist, I do not promote a certain pattern of sleep, although I do promote the idea of enough sleep. I listen to the parents. If they express that they are having a sleep-related problem, I help them analyze their values and their situation, and I give them some information from various sleep researchers. They usually come up with their own solutions. A very helpful finding by British researcher Ian St. James-Roberts and his colleagues (St. James-Roberts et al., 2006) reported in *Pediatrics* supports the benefits of responsive high-contact care during the day combined with structured independent sleep at night. They found that the infants of parents who combined a low-contact style of daytime parenting with low-contact nighttime parenting had infants who slept well, but cried more during their waking hours. The researchers also found that the parents they studied who were highly responsive to their infants and did a fair amount of holding during the day, but who provided a bedtime routine with infants sleeping in their own cribs, had babies who cried less at night and slept more than infants who were held most of the day and slept in their parents' beds at night. (See box Sleep Time Is Not Playtime for some of Magda Gerber's practical advice on sleeping.)

Sleep Time Is Not Playtime

One of Magda's practical pieces of advice to parents about sleep was to be really, really boring when responding to a baby's night waking. If Mommy shows a happy face at 2:00 a.m., baby will expect a prolonged interaction, even playtime. An uninteresting and sleepy face will show the baby that it is not playtime. Even if it takes thespian skills from an adoring new mother to feign boredom at the sight of her baby, it is in the interest of the baby's eventual self-regulation to act bored.

Feeding

As a new mother, I remember when my first child first started eating regular food, I called my mother in a panic, saying, "How will I know what to feed him?" My mother reassuringly said, "Oh, you will just know." When I asked Magda the same question, she replied, "Well, what does he like?" It sounds obvious, but at the time, it was a good reminder of a couple of things. One was that the best way to care for my child was to know him well. The second was that I needed to be responsible about what foods he was exposed to, or he would develop bad eating habits. In this culture, that is much easier said than done. As Magda once said about feeding: Adults decide *what* and *when*, and the children decide *if* and *how much*. How much clearer of a guideline could one ask for?

A reasonable approach to feeding is to give babies and young children whatever foods they like. However, this can backfire if the foods they have access to are unhealthy; salt, sugar, and excess fats are seductive. As with so many things, the most difficult part is for parents to discipline themselves. If adults want children to learn to love fresh fruits and vegetables, lean protein sources, and whole grains, that is what they must make available—and model the enjoyment of. However, if children know when they refuse these foods the parents will give them the junk food kept in the refrigerator, bad habits are reinforced, which may have serious health consequences down the road.

Childhood obesity is a genuine worry. Well-informed adults know there are many factors that contribute to it. Some are large issues that will take a consensus of society to mitigate, like poverty, unsafe neighborhoods, and advertising to children. Even too little sleep and air conditioning may be culprits, according to a recent study (Keith et al., 2006). However, on a day-to-day basis, one thing that can be done, if worked at hard enough, is to control young children's access to unhealthy food choices. (All this is said with the full recognition that families in low-income neighborhoods often do not have access to the best fresh foods. However, canned peaches are still healthier than potato chips.) There are many resources on child nutrition available, so I will leave nutritional advice about what to feed to those experts. How to feed is the area in which the RIE approach can be uniquely helpful.

Feeding Infants

The relationship-building function of feeding an infant is an obvious one. Feeding an infant in a way that is warmly interactive sets up an association in the mind–body of the baby between the psychological nourishment of love and the physical nourishment of the food. Said simply, a baby will learn that needs are met best by loving social interaction, more than by objects. Propping a bottle for an infant to self-feed gives the opposite message. Spoon feeding several infants at once lined up in high chairs also makes the food more important than the person because the infant does not get sufficiently personal attention. The reason often given for group feeding infants is timing; everybody should eat lunch at 11:30 a.m., for instance. There are logistical problems to be solved, of course. The problems, however, are worth solving because, if the goal is to promote attachment between the child and the caregiver, having one-on-one mealtimes is an important element of a child care program.

Infants cannot read the clock, and food can be kept warm somehow. When a predictable feeding rhythm can be established, infants will learn to wait until their turn to have that doubly special time with their primary carer. At The Pikler Institute, infants are always fed in the same order so that they learn the pattern. Although an infant may not be happy about having to wait, the value of the one-to-one interaction is more profound than the speed at which his hunger is addressed. Infants actually learn self-regulation from the waiting, as long as they have a general idea how long they usually have to wait. (Chaotic changes in schedule, however, undermine this important self-regulatory practice.)

How can adults make feeding infants peaceful and pleasurable? They can do this by following the same principles described in the bathing process. Have everything ready: food, drink, bibs, cloths for cleaning hands and face. Everything needed is placed on a table next to a comfortable, but not rocking, chair. Hold the baby on the lap, supporting the spine and neck, at an angle that makes visual contact attainable and swallowing safe and comfortable. Hold the bottle or spoon up just above the baby's eye level and give her a chance to decide if and when to open her mouth, speaking quietly to her about what is being offered, what her reactions are, how she seems to be feeling. Always wait until the baby shows you she is ready for the next spoonful, which is generally demonstrated by the baby

by opening her mouth or removing her thumb. Pace is determined by the
baby; sometimes the adult has to hurry to keep up, sometimes she has to
slow down. Also, a certain amount of time is devoted to each child's feeding, even if the child does not eat much. A time of relaxed communication
is as important to the baby as the calories and other nutrients at feeding
time. Love, peacefully communicated, is the best digestive aid known to
humankind.

The most important thing for an adult to remember when feeding a
baby is that only the baby can know when he or she has had enough.
Coaxing the baby to eat "just one more bite" is coercive and teaches the
baby to disengage his highly sensitive internal feedback system. There are
many physiological processes involved in appetite, and they are very efficient, even in young infants, and are probably more efficient than adults',
which have likely been interfered with. It is really, really difficult for most
adults to respect infants in this way, for myriad personal and societal reasons. It is worth the effort when adults determine to retrain their
impulses, though, because infants are internally programmed to eat when
hungry and stop eating when they have consumed enough. A healthy
infant in the context of healthy attachments will almost always eat and
drink the right amount for his biological needs without coaxing. The overall goal is for the food to meet the infant's biological needs and for adults'
attentiveness and caring to meet his psychological needs.

When a baby is able to put herself into a sitting position, usually
during early toddlerhood, it is a good time to transition her to a low table
and chair. Even better is the type of "weaning chair" used at The Pikler
Institute because it is like a tiny one-person restaurant booth. Toddlers can
climb in and out of it independently, yet the table is attached to the
bench, so they cannot push backward, the way they are inclined to do
when sitting on a stool or small chair. (It is so fun to test the adult's
patience this way!) The important points with using a low table and chair
are (a) that the toddler's feet should be able to rest comfortably on the
floor so that she feels in control of her body and well grounded, and
(b) that she continues to receive the adult's undivided attention. It is still
a one-on-one activity until she is able to self-feed. The adult's full attention scaffolds keeping the child's full attention on the task at hand. This,
again, is an instance of "wants something" quality time.

Feeding Toddlers

When two children in a group have mastered the one-on-one weaning
chair routine, they can be put together to eat, usually after they are 18
months old and are able to say a few words. This gives them the opportunity to have a bit of structured social interaction with a peer and to learn

to share the adult's attention, which will now be divided between the two children. Their skill at pouring their juice from a small pitcher, and serving themselves from the serving dish can be supported without too much disruption. When a pair of toddlers is ready, they can be joined by another toddler of similar skills, and then another. A group of no more than four toddlers is ideal. A key to success in group dining is that the adult should stay with them, remaining attentive and attuned.

Anyone who has experience sharing meal or snack time with a small group of toddlers knows the inherent pleasure and rich learning opportunities of the activity, especially in language learning. Although topics of conversation may start out tied to the objects and activities associated with mealtime, eventually, the sky's the limit and one finds out many wonderful things about a toddler's life at the table—like how many hippopotamuses were at the zoo, or what kind of airplane they got for their birthday. Readiness is an important part of the success of group activities of any sort.

As Magda often pointed out in discussions about feeding infants, there is more to be gained by the infant from one-on-one mealtimes than being lost in the shuffle of a group experience. Our own memories of family mealtimes are almost always after the age of 4 or 5. In Magda's ideal scenario, it is not appropriate to have young children at the adult dinner table before they can participate in real conversations. I always thought it was her European background that kept her from fully understanding the American value of the family dinner hour with its mild chaos and lively conversation. She and I had friendly discussions about this difference. Parents I work with often feel they want to include their babies in the family dinner. As was pointed out by researchers in Hawaii, who studied diverse groups in that location, the typical Anglo American family dinner, where the baby is pulled up to the table in the high chair and allowed to fend for herself while everyone else does the same, may be an important cultural learning experience in how loud to yell to get one's needs met (Martini, 2002).

That scenario probably would not meet program standards for most child care programs, although it may actually work fine for some families if dinner is early enough. However, eating at 7:00 or 7:30 p.m. is very late for infants and toddlers. They are usually hungry by 5:00 or 5:30 p.m., and would then be ready for bed by 7:30 p.m. Babies and toddlers will do their best to accommodate their parents. They will try to "keep it together" for a late dinner and later bedtime, but it is really better for them to eat earlier and go to bed earlier (Gerber, 2002).

For anyone who has attended or observed the banana and chamomile tea (or water) snack at RIE parent–infant classes, this may sound like a contradiction because the group of older infants are invited to join the snack table for a simple group experience. It is amazing to see how interested they are in participating. It is sometimes a little difficult to manage a group of young toddlers, as they are just learning that they must let their hands be washed, allow the bib to be put on, and sit at the table to eat. From my observations, and from the parents I work with daily, it seems as though the majority of infants and toddlers are allowed, even encouraged, to eat absolutely anywhere while walking around or playing. This is neither safe nor is it helpful in establishing mindful and healthful eating habits. Mindless eating is entrenched in our culture, unfortunately.

Although I am not against having a treat at the zoo, for instance, habitually using food to transition toddlers from one place or activity to another is an unhealthy use of food, although it is done all the time. Transitions are small stressors for toddlers and the adults who have to manage them. Using food to distract from these minor daily sensations of discomfort sets up an association between food and stress that might have unfortunate long-term consequences in how they manage stress throughout life.

In reshaping the "dining behavior" of the infants and toddlers at RIE and Pacific Oaks, my colleagues and I rely on the parents or each other to gently usher toddlers back to the table with their bananas. Snack is an important relationship-building event between the facilitator/teacher and the children. I enjoy the opportunity to be known, and loved, as the banana giver as well as the dispute facilitator. It makes sense to say, "The food stays at the table" so that little ones can come and go at first. If the food stays at the table, eventually they stay so they can eat.

Parents benefit from seeing facilitators or teachers set expectations in a respectful yet firmly consistent way as the personal and social skills that go along with eating in a group are taught. Parents are usually amazed that their toddlers will behave so maturely in class, and they often take the cue to begin setting some limits and holding up some age-appropriate expectations for their children at home. We stay calm, keep our voices low, make our requests for their cooperation politely, and trust that the children will, over time, learn to enjoy following the rules. It is so easy to get the message across when food is involved. There is little room for misinterpretation when we say, "I will give you more banana when you are sitting [i.e., not standing] on your stool." No big commands

or demands are necessary; a simple if/then or when/then w
charm. In addition, the same request is not said over and o\
dren. It is assumed they heard us the first or at least the sec
they balk, and protest because they either are not used to be
to sit while eating or they simply must test, that is okay, but
get a banana unless they are sitting. I make occasional rare (
the extremely slow-to-warm-up child, who may be allowed to sit in his
parent's lap at the table for a while.

It really is a great chance to show parents that toddlers can actually be
quite in charge of their behavior and to emphasize that the process is
more important than the performance. There are some children who
would rather play than eat, and they are not required to join, but the great
majority get on the bandwagon. They often sit as soon as the table is set
up, or even point out when the facilitator is falling down on the job. If the
facilitator does not notice the time, some young person will invariably
point at the kitchen door and say, "Ba'na?" and she knows it is time to
get hopping.

The children at RIE have made it clear that routine is a pathway that
leads to the joy of being able to anticipate pleasurable events, to the
development of the important ability to wait for delayed gratification
(e.g., nobody gets banana until everyone's hands have been cleaned and
bibs put on), and to the security of knowing the rules, few that there are.
Routine provides a framework so that each day need not be a new invention, but is an opportunity to fine tune one's orientation to the world. It
takes on the spirit of beloved ritual that nurtures relationships as much as
bodies.

References

Brazleton, T. B. (1992). *Working and caring.* New York: Perseus Books.

Brown, M. W. (1947). *Goodnight moon.* New York: Harper.

Chess, S., & Thomas, A. (1987). *Know your child: An authoritative guide for today's parents.* New York: Basic Books.

Copple, C., & Bredekamp, S. (Eds.). (2009). *Developmentally appropriate practice in early childhood programs serving children from birth through age 8* (3rd ed.). Washington, DC: National Association for the Education of Young Children.

Coukell, A. (2006, May 30). Dr. Ferber revisits his "crying baby" theory. *Day to day* [Radio program]. Washington, DC: National Public Radio.

Erikson, E. H. (1950). *Childhood and society.* New York: W. W. Norton & Co.

Ferber, R. (1985). *Solve your child's sleep problems.* New York: Simon & Schuster.

Ferber, R. (2006). *Solve your child's sleep problems* (Rev. ed.). New York: Simon & Schuster.

rber, M. (Ed.). (1979). *The RIE manual for parents and professionals.* Los Angeles: Resources for Infant Educarers.

Gerber, M. (2002). *Dear parent: Caring for infants with respect* (expanded edition). Los Angeles: Resources for Infant Educarers.

Gonzalez-Mena, J. (2008). *Diversity in early care and education: Honoring differences.* New York: McGraw-Hill.

Gonzalez-Mena, J., & Widmeyer Eyer, D. (2008). *Infants, toddlers and caregivers, (8th ed.).* New York: McGraw Hill.

Keith, S. W., Redden, D. T., Katzmarzyk, P. T., Boggiano, M. M., Hanlon, E. C., Benca, R. M., et al. (2006). Putative contributors to the secular increase in obesity: Exploring the roads less traveled. *International Journal of Obesity, 30,* 1585–1594.

Martini, M. (2002). How mothers in four American cultural groups shape infant learning during mealtimes. *Zero to Three, 22*(4), 14–20.

Oxford American Dictionary & Thesaurus. (1996). New York: Dorling Kindersley & Oxford University Press.

Perry, B. D. (2004). Understanding traumatized and maltreated children: The core concepts. *ChildTrauma Academy Educator's Package: Series 1 CD-ROM.* Houston, TX: ChildTrauma Academy.

Sears, W. (1985). *Nighttime parenting: How to get your baby and child to sleep.* Franklin Park, IL: La Leche League International.

Small, M. (1998). *Our babies, ourselves: How culture and biology shape the way we parent.* New York: Anchor Books.

St. James-Roberts, I., Alvarez, M., Csipke, E., Abramsky, T., Goodwin, J., & Sorgenfrei, E. (2006). Infant crying and sleeping in London, Copenhagen and when parents adopt a "proximal" form of care. *Pediatrics, 117,* e1146–e1155.

Tardos, A. (1996, May). *Disciplining toddlers.* Paper presented at the pre-RIE Conference evening for RIE Associates, Los Angeles.

Tardos, A., & Appell, G. (1992). *Paying attention to each other: Infant and adult during the bath* [DVD]. Budapest, Hungary: The Pikler Institute.

Weissbluth, M. (1999). *Healthy sleep habits, happy child.* New York: Ballantine Books.

Chapter 3

Setting the Stage: How to Make the Environment a Partner

How to order a comfortable caregiving area as well as safe space in which infants are free to move and play without interference is one of the helpful messages of RIE. Most environments have inherent pluses and minuses. However, there are things people can do to give the baby opportunities to maximize the use of space, time, and resources, however limited, to the baby's and adult's benefit.

*I*t was doctor's orders. My mother was getting ready to put boric acid solution in my eyes. I was crying at the top of my newborn lungs, the dog was standing between her legs at the bathroom sink wagging his tail, and my 3½-year-old brother was in the room trying to get her attention at his usual, exuberant decibel level. She reached for what she thought was the bottle of boric acid, but instead grabbed a bottle of rubbing alcohol, and started pouring. You can imagine the pain I experienced, and the horror my poor mother felt when she realized what she had done. Later, the doctor told her she had reacted correctly, by using the boric acid to wash out the alcohol. It was one of her worst maternal memories. To this day, I suspect that I carry the memory of that mishap in chronically tense shoulder muscles.

Another mishap that happened to me when I was an infant was when, one day, I was lying on the couch, obviously still too young to roll over. My brother, who thought I was wonderful, came in from playing and bent over to kiss me. That would have been a lovely scene, except that his toy six-shooter fell out of his holster (it was the '50s, by the way) and landed right between my eyes. The cut it made on the bridge of my nose bled profusely, and my brother felt terrible that he had hurt me. I have the scar to this day. I think of it as a testament to my brother's early affection for me, but that event has probably also taken up residence in my tense shoulders as well.

Was it simply parental error that allowed me to suffer those two injuries? Maybe, but what parent or caregiver is able to foresee and avert all mishaps? Few indeed. That is why it is so important to make the environment a partner. Having a caregiving area set up in a place to which other children, or dogs, do not have access will allow the adult to focus his or her attention on the care of the one child. A gate at the bathroom door of my house might have given my mother the calm space and ability to focus that would have helped her reach for the correct bottle.

In a family setting, more creative effort is required to provide focused attention to one child because the excluded sibling (if there is only one) might feel really shut out and frustrated. A 2-year-old might not be able to handle being "put away" on the other side of a gate every time the new baby needs to feed. If there are more children, there may be no such place as a "perfectly safe" area when talking about a home with, for instance, a newborn, a 2- and a 5-year-old, especially when the mother is the only adult present. This is truly on-the-job pressure. So in the home, it makes sense for older siblings to be allowed to be nearer to their mother while she's nursing the baby. They can learn to accommodate this new call on mother's attention, and learn to respect the needs of the baby. Hopefully, the baby will receive enough focused attention to feel appreciated, without there being too much jealousy on the part of the older sibling(s). A nice, helpful activity is to share with the older siblings baby pictures of themselves so that they can be reminded that they received special attention when they were babies, too.

The pain of exclusion during someone else's special time with the caregiver is less in child care. Being in a group affords the children a sense of belonging, even when their beloved caregiver is attending to another child. Even young babies enjoy the presence of peers and seem to experience this as meaningful togetherness. With regard to standards for supervision in child care settings, fortunately there are often enough adults present so that when one is concentrating on changing a diaper, another is available to observe the others in the room. A team approach to primary care is a good model: There is a special person for each child, but there are also secondary familiar adults with whom the child is comfortable.

There is no way a carer can change one baby's diaper with focused attention if another one is tugging on her knees; neither can she feed a baby a bottle as peacefully as the baby deserves if other children are climbing on her back. An ideal environment would always have an adjacent gated area for caregiving activities, which gives the adult a view of the room but still affords separation from the group during care. Fortunately, even when the space is not ideal, creative solutions are possible. Ruth Money, who opened the first RIE-certified child care center, the South Bay Infant Center in Redondo Beach, California, met the challenge of creating a caregiving space separate from the play area by putting a comfy chair in a playpen for the educarer to sit in to feed one infant while the other children had the run of the rest of the room.

How can you safely leave the play area to care for one baby, leaving the others playing together? You may think that sounds like a recipe for disaster. That is why having a safe place to put a baby down that protects her from the mistakes of older children is essential. This is especially imperative in a mixed-age child care setting.

A parent in one of my RIE classes told me the following story.

Her son, Ethan, who was only 3 months old, was enrolled in a well-regarded corporate child care center. One day she went to pick him up and found his face covered with scratches. He was in a room with newborns to 18-month-olds. The older ones were supposed to have moved on to a new classroom, but there was not room yet. Ethan's classroom was really not set up for such a wide age range. Within the first few days in care, one of the toddlers had grabbed Ethan's face, drawing blood. The same thing happened the next day. When she told me about this during our Saturday parent–infant class, I suggested she bring a playpen to the center for her son to play in until the older toddlers had moved on. She thought that sounded like a good plan, so she offered that solution to the teachers at the center.

The head teacher responded, "Oh, no. We are a RIE-based program, and we don't use playpens!" I was horrified to hear this misinterpretation of the RIE message. A playpen is a perfect place for a baby to play in until he starts rolling over and over. A playpen would have offered Ethan freedom of movement in a safe space while not placing developmentally inappropriate expectations on the toddlers to control their exploratory impulses. The rearrangement of the space and use of appropriate safety equipment would have provided the necessary restrictions when teachers were busy with other tasks. In the end, I think the mother ended up removing Ethan from that program. It would probably have been a great place for him while she was working, but this safety issue soured his mother to the other possibilities the center might have offered.

It is not enough to make sure electrical outlets are covered and that there are no stray push pins on the floor. Having a truly safe environment means that the play area is arranged so that exploration can happen even when adults' eyes are occupied elsewhere (Gerber, 2002). Of course, supervision is essential. Realistically, however, super-vision means seeing the big picture, not necessarily seeing every moment of every child's day. Even the most vigilant of carers (parent or professional) cannot have their eyes trained on a baby 100% of its waking hours. However, in addition to the usual safety measures inherent in licensing standards, there are some important elements of a RIE environment that make it possible to provide focused attention during care as well as a safe play place for the others who are neither sleeping nor receiving care.

The first principle is to provide separate play areas for small groups of children of similar abilities, placing crawlers with crawlers, walkers with walkers, except when special developmental needs dictate otherwise. This assures that bigger/older/more able children cannot overwhelm smaller/younger/less able ones. When infants and toddlers are well matched in their gross motor skills, they can be left together without constant interference or intervention by adults. This allows the adults to give undivided attention to one child at a time during caregiving, and it allows the infants and toddlers to feel that they are trusted when they are on their own for a little while, building their self-confidence. Infants and toddlers in groups can learn to be content to play without adult direction while their caregivers are busy with other children if they are not worried that they will be overpowered by bigger children. When caregivers know their children's capabilities, they can learn to feel comfortable, thus allowing independent play if the separate areas for caregiving have visual access to the play areas.

To create a safe yet interesting play space, use modular climbing equipment that can be geared to the skill level of the particular group. More challenging pieces can be added as the children master easier pieces. (This is a topic that is discussed more in chapter 6.) In family home child care situations, where adult-sized furniture cannot easily be removed, creative solutions and special care in ensuring that heavy furniture is securely bolted are essential. Removable gates or play fences can eliminate access to forbidden temptations like entertainment equipment.

Facilitators at RIE recommend letting infants and toddlers learn to move on hard surfaces like a thin rug, wood floor, or linoleum. Too much cushioning inhibits their ability to find their balance and learn their limits. If a baby is always put on a rug or padded floor, she will have no motivation to learn to protect her head when rolling over. A small hurt, like the surprise of rolling over the first time to find solid ground under one's head, is a learning experience that may seem like a trauma to a parent or caregiver, but it is really an important opportunity to develop body awareness and knowledge of the environment. Spending most of the time on a thickly padded floor while learning to get along in gravity is not what helps a new person find equilibrium. After the child is walking well on solid ground, then learning to stay balanced while walking on a squishy padded surface can be an interesting new challenge. In *The Origins of Free Play*, Kálló and Balog (2005) quoted Emmi Pikler as saying, "We too prefer dancing on parquet floors to dancing on mattresses" (p.62).

From the time they are around 3 months old, after they have discovered their hands, the infants at The Pikler Institute are placed on their backs on a wooden floor covered with a cotton sheet that can be tied to the uprights of the playpen. They do not develop persistently flat heads, contrary to a fear that seems to be a newly prevalent worry for parents in the United States since the Back to Sleep campaign was first introduced by the American Academy of Pediatrics ("Back to Sleep Policy Statement," 2005). A controlled study was conducted in France (Cavalier & Picaud, 2008) to compare the incidence of positional plagiocephaly between babies whose parents either did or did not have information about the importance of freedom of movement as taught by Pikler (and RIE). They found no evidence of a relationship between sleeping position and the condition, but that not allowing infants to move freely was more likely implicated.

RIE and Pikler babies are always placed on their backs and are free to move as they are internally motivated to do. They tend to change position on average about once per minute (Roche, 1994). These infants are not subjected to infant seats and other restrictive equipment (Gerber, 1979) except during car trips, which are kept to a minimum. Swings, carseats, other infant carriers, and bolsters with Velcro that keep them on their backs constitute for many infants fairly constant microenvironments that do not permit freedom to move. In them, infants are locked in positions where adjustments for comfort or stimulation are impossible. These sorts of restraints may be a culprit in causing molding of the skull, not to mention learned passivity. Barring rare congenital difficulties, such as torticollis, infants who are allowed plenty of time to move freely without restraint do not develop abnormally flattened heads.

Description of the RIE Center Environment

As an example of how a space not built with infants and toddlers in mind can be adapted for their use, I describe the original RIE Center, where our parent–infant classes were held for 20 years. It was located in the downstairs unit of Magda Gerber's duplex on a small circular street on the top of a hill, in a neighborhood just northeast of downtown Los Angeles called Silverlake. Imagine when you walk inside, you enter the living room, which is used as a place to leave shoes and diaper bags during class, and as a classroom for adult RIE education, a very humble and cozy space with natural light and hardwood floors. There is a low barrier made of wooden cubes separating the living room and the play room, which was originally the dining room of the apartment. In this play area, there is a door to the kitchen on the right and a door to the bathroom and offices (originally bedrooms) on the left, which were both latched during class.

The inside classroom, the smallish dining room, which is painted off-white, includes a round heather blue braided rug, which is not padded, on a hardwood floor. There is a nook, painted sky blue, to the left with a twin bed-sized mattress and bolsters for lounging. There is an observation window from the back bedroom out of the line of the children's sight. On the

wall to the right, by the kitchen, there are three open wooden 18-inch cubes for toy shelves. In the middle cube, a circle has been cut out of the top of the open cube, and usually a plastic colander with some toys in it is placed in the hole. This hole becomes the focus of lots and lots of in-and-out play—first with toys and then with whole bodies. On either side of the wide doorway to the sun porch are vertical window openings (no glass) with sills low enough to create a place for toddlers, and even very adventurous babies, to learn to climb in and out.

Beyond the main play area is a narrow sun porch, with a changing table on the right and French doors that lead to a covered redwood deck. Large trees make the deck a lovely, shady, and peaceful area. (Magda always told us the trees were magical.) Unless the weather is cold or rainy, the French doors are latched open so that the babies or toddlers get to choose where they will play. This is a luxury in Southern California most residents are able to take for granted.

Most of the sealed redwood deck is covered by ½ inch thick blue-and-white interlocking rubber tiles that are very firm. Parents sit on comfortable Backjack floor chairs around the perimeter of the inside or outside play area. As a facilitator, I prefer to sit on a Zen meditation pillow, as it helps me sit comfortably yet be able to move easily in any direction. The floor chairs lean too far back for the spontaneous mobility needed by a facilitator.

The youngest infants start out, usually, on the rug or rubber tiles, which are both covered with a sheet so spit-up or other bodily fluids can be easily washed out. They venture out gradually as they learn to move through space. The environment will eventually include 4- or 6-inch platforms, low ramps, tunnels, or stair steps in the arrangement as the infants become ready for them. (How to tell when they are ready is discussed in chapter 6.)

Play objects, which may or may not be designed as toys, are chosen by the facilitator depending on the ages and abilities of the infants or toddlers in each group. As the children come only once a week for 1½–2 hours, RIE facilitators are very slow to make changes in the setup because children benefit from learning to know what to expect in the environment. Only after it has been observed for a few weeks that particular toys are not generating interest will these toys be replaced with others. A constantly changing play environment promotes dabbling rather than deep engagement. The goal at RIE is to promote the creativity needed to make the present objects interesting rather than the consumerism of needing new objects all of the time. Magda always said a little boredom inspires initiative.

The standard RIE guideline for how many play objects are needed for a group is very simple: There should be 3 or 4 objects, or sets of objects, for each child in the group. So, a class of seven infants would need no more than 21 to 28 objects (or sets like stacking cups). It is always better to start out with fewer, and add things, than to start out with too much. The youngest infants may not really even be ready for toys; their hands and their own bodies are what they need to play with. (Some suggestions of items for various age groups are included in chapter 7.) Something in each of the three cubes, a group of toys in the basket filling the hole, a bin full of balls, a few dolls, some climbing equipment, and *voilá!* it is a great place for a group of crawling babies.

There have never been more than one or two pieces of simple artwork on the walls of the play area, just above a cruising baby's eye level. Having too busy a visual environment does not create that peaceful, open-minded "What shall I do now?" feeling Magda always encouraged. Infants have so much to attend to in a group setting, most notably one another, so the intention is not to overwhelm their senses. (Waldorf, Montessori, and Reggio classrooms are often exemplary in this aspect.) When asked by parents how they should decorate the nursery, Magda's advice was to make it a pleasant place for the adults, so they would want to be with the children in that space. I would add that an aesthetically pleasing decor shows respect for the baby. An overemphasis on "cute" things, to me, is a little insulting, a sort of visual baby-talk. I feel strongly that Magda's suggestion for decorating a baby's bedroom applies to a classroom or child care setting as well. Being surrounded by too many bright primary colors all day can be overstimulating; it would be like living in a fast food restaurant. When I see an infant or toddler room all done up in Disney characters or cartoonish murals, I worry that the children will be deprived of more nuanced stimulation on so many levels. Parents and other caring adults often buy many toys for young children out of the best of motives, but the people who market toys are much more concerned with their profit than with whether or not their products are actually good for children (Linn, 2004). It has been my observation over the years that children who have too many things have a harder time playing peacefully and learning to share than children who have less. Maybe in their minds they have a hard time discerning how much is "enough." If a person wants to give a gift to a child that lasts forever, the child would be better served if the person offers his or her time rather than some object that will probably soon be meaningless to the child.

Quietude as the Baseline

In discussing the environment of a RIE classroom, one must consider above everything the social–emotional environment. The attitude of the adults in the room contributes more to the ambience than any other element. Quiet observation of the infants' play makes psychic space for them to explore and delve deeply into their inquiries because they do not have to waste energy screening out irrelevant chatter or keeping one part of their minds on such things as, "Is she talking about me? What is she saying?" In addition, they do not need a running commentary on their activities, however much teachers and parents want to support their language development.

When observing during program time, I wait until the child looks up at me to invite my response to his activity before making a comment. Then, a descriptive statement is welcome, and possibly even informative, rather than intrusive. The exception to this point is when I use "sportscasting," or descriptive narration to head off conflicts when multiple children are in close quarters, which is discussed at further length in chapter 8.

In promoting the value of quiet observation of children's play, I do not want to overlook the fact that even young children benefit from alone time, or at least from a sense of psychological privacy (Gerber, 2002). Babies can occupy themselves without adults being there, although some are naturally more independent than others. Later, around the time they become sufficiently verbal to carry on an internal or external private dialogue in their play, there is a point at which older toddlers start to express self-consciousness when adults are watching. After a child reaches this stage, it is still possible to observe obliquely, and be available when needed, without the child feeling overly scrutinized. There will, of course, be those times when children request an adult's attention and appreciation of their new accomplishments. As always, sustaining optimal attunement requires sensitivity on the part of the adult.

Music in the Air

There is one subject that always comes up with infant–toddler teachers, which is related to the notion of making an environment pleasant for the adult workers: How much and what kind of music should be played in the classroom? Music is the result of a basic human impulse, and no one would dispute its importance in the lives of children, but humans were not designed to have electronically generated music coming at them all day long. However, many adults are accustomed to having a radio or CD playing in the background all of the time. This makes them feel comfortable and connected to the outside world, so they play it in their infant–toddler classrooms for their own entertainment. Others think, on behalf of the children, "If some is good, more is better." However, a judicious use of music is more consistent with the RIE approach.

Too much input and the nervous system overloads, at which point the brain must start to screen out incoming stimuli. The RIE approach involves creating an environment from which infants and toddlers do not need to retreat on an ongoing basis. High-quality music of different kinds should be provided for infants and toddlers at specific times, at a volume that is not too loud and for a duration that holds their attention. In digestible doses, it is a wonderful gift to share one's musical passions with children. They can and do appreciate many styles and genres besides children's music. (When asked "What shall we sing now?" during singing time, one of the toddlers in my class once suggested his favorite song, "When Doves Cry" by Prince!)

Infants' and toddlers' senses are as keen as they will ever be, and their discernment of subtlety is highly developed. There is research that indicates that, in the same way that they are most primed to learn the basic elements of language and face recognition in the first year of life, they are most capable of internalizing complicated rhythmic patterns in their first year (Hannon & Trehub, 2005). This finding suggests that it is important to expose young children to diverse types of music. However, an all-day auditory diet is too much. When adults are sharing space with children, they must not assume that because they personally like to have music playing all the time that it is good for the children. An appropriately "tidy" auditory environment is just as important as a visually tidy environment. Turning up the volume too high is another frequent mistake adults make when sharing music with young children. This is jarring to the nervous system, especially for sensitive children (Williamson & Anzalone, 2002), and can be harmful to their hearing.

All great promoters in show business know that you have to leave an audience wanting more, which applies to infants and toddlers the same as it does to adults. In the course of a child care day, I would recommend no more than three or four 10–15 minute periods of music. (Nap music should be turned off once the children are asleep, for a deeper rest.) Whenever possible, include live music; that is what human beings evolved with: If people wanted music, they had to make it. Making music by singing with children is a lovely way to build relationships as well as vocabularies and musical intelligence. If instruments can be included, so much the better. It is important for children to learn early that people make music, not electronic devices.

The Outdoors

Access to the beauty and freedom of the natural world should be every child's right, and even the youngest babies respond favorably to being outside. At The Pikler Institute, from the youngest to the oldest, each group of children has complete environments both indoors and outdoors. They eat, sleep, are diapered, and play outside to the fullest extent weather permits. Each child has a bed inside and a bed outside. Napping infants outdoors in winter is a common practice in very cold climates; it is seen as an important way to help acclimatize a baby to the environment into which he has been born. Icelandic babies are regularly bundled up to nap in their prams on the front porch in the wintertime. A German friend of mine once told me, "There's no such thing as bad weather; there are just the wrong clothes."

Of course it is imperative to protect children from too much exposure to direct sun or other harsh elements, but it is also important to realize that adults can overprotect them, too. Toddlers are less likely to engage in conflict outdoors. This may be because there are often more exciting physical challenges (e.g., uneven ground, places to climb and run) and more interesting tactile sensory stimulation (e.g., sand, grass, swaying trees, bark) in play yards than indoors. It may also be that the claustrophobic effects of being enclosed in four walls, a ceiling, and a floor, however roomy, may jangle at children's nerves. Sounds reverberate less outside. Natural light lifts moods. Greenery soothes. The research makes clear that there are many developmental benefits children receive by having access to nature (Louv, 2006; Wells, 2000; Wells & Evans, 2003).

In one of my RIE classes, I have a toddler, Lucie, who seemed very timid, almost always staying very close to her mother during class. She would make verbal and eye contact, sharing her pleasure in the toys with the adults during class. She would occasionally venture forth to explore, but whenever other toddlers came close, she usually retreated to her mother's lap. The group had been meeting once a week for 90 minutes in my indoor classroom for more than 1½ years, from the time the toddlers were only a few weeks old. When they were all nearing 2, I decided I would move the class to the outdoor area, adding the complexity of water, sand, and rocks—a major change in venue. The change in attitude Lucie displayed was really astounding. She sat in the sand area and shoveled sand into the same bucket with another child. She stood at the sinks and laughed with Sam as he squirted water onto her by placing his hand over the faucet. She smiled at her mother but stayed where she was. The only way I could account for the change was that outside she felt safer.

The question may arise as to why it took me so long to take them outside. The main emphasis of the 90-minute RIE Parent–Infant Guidance class was twofold. First was to allow the parents to learn to observe their infants' competencies in moving and playing within a prepared environment and to explore topics the parents wished to discuss. Second was to give the infants a chance to play freely with one another and learn to be comfortable with peers. By going outside too soon, the group experience would have been diluted by the wide open spaces. Intimacy would be lost, and physical safety would have taken up too much of my attention because the yard is more amenable to walking toddlers than crawling babies. Although crawling babies do enjoy exploring the yard, they spend much less time interacting with one another in that space than they do inside. In my hierarchy of values, as they only have one chance per week to connect with the group, I wanted more of a social "pressure cooker" at first. When they are older, bigger, and more mobile, the outdoor environment provides a backdrop that allows for exploration of the natural as well as the social environment. What is lost in intimacy is gained in the expansiveness of the open sky. For Lucie, the pressure inside was obviously too much. She was much happier with the lid off.

When children are in a group all day, getting the lid off the social pressure cooker is something that must happen regularly. Free access to the outdoors is ideal, when the indoor and outdoor spaces are contiguous. Arranging staffing so someone is available to be outside and someone else is inside can be negotiated among the team. Including rain gear for children in furnishing the classroom will quell parental worries about children getting wet. Educarers must also be comfortably outfitted to supervise in inclement weather. The evidence is overwhelming: Toddlers have more fun in mud puddles than at Disneyland. Infants may not need to be out in the rain, of course, but a covered patio that gives the opportunity to experience fresh air and visual access, at least, to natural surroundings will make long days in care more enjoyable and less stressful.

Taking a Walk

There is a child care center with a lovely outdoor setting down the block from the Pacific Oaks Infant–Toddler/Parent Center. Often while preparing snacks, I see babies from this other center being wheeled by in their six-pack stroller, or the toddlers being taken on a walk by their caregivers. I see the toddler group shuffling along our driveway in a double line, each child holding onto a rope, with adults herding from either end, talking to each other over the toddlers' heads. I always feel sad for those toddlers. Perhaps the purpose is to train them in case of fire or other emergencies, which may be wise. Hopefully, however, the adults do not fool themselves that this is a wonderful piece of curricular enrichment, because it does not give the toddlers the opportunity for discovery in any tangible sense. To me, children holding a rope in a group seem like little soldiers, not little explorers. On the other hand, there is a way to take a walk with toddlers that is practiced at The Pikler Institute that I wish every child care teacher and administrator could observe and replicate.

At The Pikler Institute, toddlers begin going on walks when they display curiosity about the world outside their house and play yard. Taking a walk with a teacher, who is not their caregiver, is a very special occasion that happens only about once or twice a week. (Remember, the children live at the institute full time.) Two children are thoughtfully paired with a compatible peer of similar interests. They may go where they like on the grounds of the institute, examining flowers, watching the handyman work, peeking into basement windows. The teacher is there to support their curiosity and to keep them safe. As the toddlers display interest in the wider world outside the gate, and if they show readiness to accept guidance from their teacher and to hold her finger while crossing the street, they will venture into the neighborhood, where there are snow banks to climb, cats and dogs to visit, cars to watch, and neighbors to greet. The walk, for which they have put on their special clothes, may take 45 minutes, and they may cover no more than half a block. The pace is determined totally by the children. Somewhat older children may have a mission on their walks, perhaps to choose a piece of candy at the corner store, or buy some apples for their group's afternoon snack. They learn about money, the types of transactions people have in daily life, and how to talk to different people. However pleasurable she may find them, these walks are not for the benefit of the teacher; they are for the children entirely, and the children are never forced to do more or go further than they desire. The adult allows the children to lead, offering guidance and information, sharing with pleasure their joy, mediating any anxieties that come up ("Yes, the dog barked at us. But he is inside the fence; he can't hurt us."). The goal is to increase the children's awareness of the world, build her confidence, and instill a sense of belonging. It is a customized experience designed to meet the needs of the individual child, and it is a joy to behold. This is an experience anyone can provide for a child, with nothing more than three quarters of an hour to spend. If time is money, it will surely be well spent.

For parents alone at home with toddlers, a walk in the neighborhood can be a welcome interlude for everyone. A very experienced mother I know described the hours of pleasure she had while walking outdoors with her toddler, who was known in the family as "The Worm Queen," a title  she relished, because after a rain, it was her mission to save all of the earthworms from being run over by passing cars. While her mother kept watch, she would lovingly pick up as many of the stranded creatures as she could and carry them to the side of the road where they could safely go back underground. She was allowed to pursue her own interests, motivated by compassion, and bond with her fellow beings of the earth, safely held in her mother's tender awareness. The combination of being outdoors with the freedom to follow a line of inquiry or intention in an unhurried way, while the adult supports and appreciates what the child is doing, builds intellect, self-awareness, and relationships in a holistic, integrated way which being herded while holding a rope never could. More interactive, even if less frequent, outings could make being in full-time child care more rewarding for children and adults.

In summary, whereas caring for infants and toddlers is always challenging work, how the environment is ordered and utilized, inside and outside, can make a long day in a group either more exhausting or more peaceful. It is possible for the environment to be a silent teammate.

References

Back to sleep policy statement. (2005). *Pediatrics, 116*(5), 1245–1255. Retrieved July 30, 2009, from http://aappolicy.aappublications.org/cgi/content/full/pediatrics;116/5/1245

Cavalier, A., & Picaud, J.-C. (2008). Prévention de la plagiocéphaie posturale (Positional plagiocephaly in primary care). *Archives de Pédiatrie, 15*, S20–S24. Retrieved August 18, 2009, from www.sciencedirect.com/science?_ob = ArticleURL&_udi = B6VKK-4THKK0C-4&_user = 8149853&_coverDate = 06%2F30%2F2008&_alid = 984306907&_rdoc = 1&_fmt = high&_orig = search&_cdi = 6125&_sort = d&_docanchor = &view = c &_ct = 2&_acct = C000050221&_version = 1&_urlVersion = 0&_userid = 8149853& md5 = 9bff95334754a15130150bcb7f0ca1be

Gerber, M. (Ed.). (1979). *The RIE manual for parents and professionals.* Los Angeles: Resources for Infant Educarers.

Gerber, M. (2002). *Dear parent: Caring for infants with respect* (expanded edition). Los Angeles: Resources for Infant Educarers.

Hannon, E., & Trehub, S. (2005). Tuning in to musical rhythms: Infants learn more readily than adults. *Proceedings of the National Academy of Sciences, 102*(35), 12639–12643.

Kálló, E., & Balog, G. (2005). *The origins of free play.* Budapest, Hungary: Pikler-Lóczy Társaság.

Linn, S. (2004). *Consuming kids: The hostile takeover of childhood.* New York: The New Press.

Louv, R. (2006). *Last child in the woods: Saving our children from nature-deficit disorder.* Chapel Hill, NC: Algonquin Books of Chapel Hill.

Roche, M. A. (Ed.). (1994). Emmi Pikler: 1902–1984. [Special issue]. *Sensory Awareness Foundation Bulletin, 14.*

Wells, N. (2000). At home with nature: Effects of "greenness" on children's cognitive functioning. *Environment and Behavior, 32*(6), 775–795.

Wells, N., & Evans, G. (2003). Nearby nature: A buffer of life stress among rural children. *Environment and Behavior, 35*(3), 311–330.

Williamson, G. G., & Anzalone, M. (2002). *Sensory integration and self-regulation in infants and toddlers: Helping very young children interact with their environment.* Washington, DC: ZERO TO THREE.

Chapter 4

Why Talk to Babies? Language and Literacy From Day One

It may seem unnecessary to talk to infants, especially for those who come from traditional cultures in which much of what passes between parents and children is contextual and nonverbal. Even highly verbal adults are often embarrassed by the idea of speaking to newborn infants as though they can understand. It feels so silly, at first, to say, "I want to pick you up now. Are you ready?" when you know the baby cannot possibly understand your words. Yet the habit of talking to a child as if she understands assures her of the opportunity to learn to understand not just words, but ideas and intentions as well (Gerber, 2002). This is particularly important when an infant or toddler is being cared for by someone from a culture different than the one to which she goes home at the end of the day.

Although RIE practitioners refrain from teaching infants how to move and how to play, infants must learn to speak from conversations with adults and older children. However, even in this important area of social learning, the RIE approach relies on the child's will to communicate, and on the adult's desire to communicate with him, rather than deliberately teaching language. What can be seen, before words are ever produced, is the turn-taking of communication (Mangione 1999). Infants who have sensitive caregivers show fantastic skill at knowing how to bounce the give-and-take back and forth with older partners (e.g., parents, caregivers, older siblings, even strangers in a restaurant), and derive great pleasure from doing so. Infants acquire language from adults speaking to them in the everyday occurrences that are the events of their lives (Meier, 2004). Unless a baby has a special need that gets in the way, he will be learning language, whether verbal or nonverbal, in every interaction.

- "Do you want milk?"

- "I'm going to pick you up now."

- "The wet wipe is cold, isn't it?"

- "Ooh, the bunny feels soft!"

- "Do you want the red cup or the yellow one?"

- "Kevin dropped the toy truck. It made a loud bang that scared you."

These are the types of sentences that help babies connect language with their immediate experience. When adults talk to babies about the things that concern them—such as what is happening to their bodies; what they are sensing with their eyes, ears, nose, mouth, and skin; what people near them are doing; and what they might be feeling about all of it—the words naturally "stick" in their minds because of the emotional meaning connected to them. Their motivation is keen; their very survival is connected to words. ("Hot!" is an easy one to remember.) What Magda Gerber stressed, which makes the RIE approach work so beautifully to foster communication skills, is not just to talk to babies, but to wait for their response. Observing what the baby does during this pause gives adults the information they need to proceed with the interaction in a way that will keep the baby engaged in the activity or conversation in progress. It is the equivalent of listening to the verbal response of an adult conversation partner. Once during an observation at a child care center that was engaged in RIE training, it was interesting to see how half of the RIE message had gotten through to the caregivers. The caregiver I observed had the part about talking during a diaper change, but she was not waiting for a response and adjusting accordingly. There may have been vocabulary being transmitted, and a sort of "fair warning" about what was going to happen, but there was not the reciprocal communication going on that I had hoped to see. If this well-meaning caregiver had waited quietly after saying, "I want to take off your pants," she might have made space for the baby to take the initiative to lift his hips up to help her. Waiting for a signal that the adult's request has been heard may seem inefficient, but slowing down allows the baby to actively participate (cooperate) rather than just passively comply.

During the first year or more, vocabulary is being learned "offline" as babies absorb language from their social environment. At some point, sufficient neural connections are made, and they go "online" and begin to reproduce words. The amount and quality of language exchanged during the offline phase will certainly affect the results when they go online, whether that is sooner or later than average. There is impressive empirical research that shows that infants and toddlers who are spoken and listened to more often have larger vocabularies at school age and perform better academically (Hart & Risley, 1995). The RIE approach to communication gets the language ball rolling from the very beginning.

The RIE approach is rooted in the Euro-American, low-context culture that depends primarily on verbal communication rather than on unspoken understandings (Hall, 1976; Hart & Risley, 1995). It builds on this value by making the assumption that even the youngest babies can understand, if not the words, at least the rudiments of the intentions of the adults who speak with them. The RIE way of giving respect through relevant conversational give-and-take right from birth lays the foundation for success in a society that requires skill and comfort in sharing ideas and feelings with a wide variety of others. Children who have been raised in a RIE-influenced environment are often remarkable for their ease in speaking unself-consciously with adults other than their close family members because they are used to having such conversations. This orientation has been described as an important element of success in a typical academic setting by Annette Lareau (2003), author of *Unequal Childhoods*. Whether this is culturally fair or not, if adults want to set children up for academic success, this type of communication in out-of-home experiences makes sense. Children who are raised in homes that operate on more nonverbal, high-context values, including many immigrant and first-generation children in this country, will benefit in child care and other out-of home contexts from experience with this explicit, highly verbal way of communicating. Consciously communicating this way may help to prepare children for entry into the mainstream educational system and may compensate for some of the cultural biases inherent in public education.

Of course, whenever possible, infants should be cared for by adults who speak the children's home language, both for the comfort of the child and for the sake of parent–carer communication. However, when this is not possible, the RIE approach to speaking with the child about his or her concerns will provide a bridge to bilingual development in a respectful and nonpressured manner.

The Role of Language in Emotional Intelligence

Another aspect of the RIE approach that makes it different from other ways of preparing children for success as communicators is its underlying respect for the emotional integrity of the child (Gerber, 2002). Magda was adamant that adults not tell young children how to feel, although she advocated that words be suggested to help them process and learn to

identify their feelings. It is impossible to talk about "language development" without also talking about what the language is repre-senting. What people speak is in many ways more impor-tant than that they speak. RIE practitioners try not to talk at children, but listen as much as talk, fishing for feelings without pronouncements because we would rather not make assumptions about what they are thinking and feeling, in case we are wrong. We often are, according to Yamamoto (1993).

- "I am not sure why you are crying. I wonder how I can help you feel better."

- "Are you frustrated with that puzzle?"

- "Mommy has gone to work. Your face looks sad. Do you want me to hold you?"

- "I think you are angry, but I won't let you hit me."

- "What a nice hug! You seem happy to see Tammy today!"

Authenticity is the key to building emotional intelligence. If an adult is irritated with the noise a child is producing banging toys, but puts on a phony face and pretends to approve, the child will be getting mixed messages. She may not quite get that the adult really does not like it, but she also will realize that a smile does not mean the adult does like it. Recognition of emotional expressions is a specialty of babies and young children because reading the caregiver's face is essential to their survival (Schore, 2003). When an adult is being honest about his feelings, as long as the feelings are not overwhelming, this helps young children make sense of the social realm. An adult's true face, and the words that match, keep the child motivated to stay in dialogue with the adult, and help the child to be psychobiologically attuned with herself and others (Schore, 1994).

Adding Language to Play

RIE practitioners do not interrupt infants' concentration on a task just to teach them words. For instance, if a baby is putting hair curlers into a large water jug, one by one, RIE practitioners do not start narrating their actions or questioning them or directing them ("Where's the yellow one? Can you put the yellow one in?"). They quietly enjoy watching the child's testing and problem solving. When babies look up to invite an acknowledgement of their activity, only then would the respectful practitioner make an appropriate comment or pose a question ("It looks like the purple ones are too big to fit. You put all the pink ones in, though!"). More on the RIE approach to play will be included in chapter 7, but it is impossible to separate language development from all the other aspects of development.

No Pressure

In the same way that infants reach certain levels of physical development at different times depending on their unique timetables, so they also begin to produce words, phrases, and sentences in their own good time. Many factors contribute to the onset of the spoken word. Obviously, the amount and quality of verbal interaction with caring adults will play a big part. The more give-and-take "conversations" adults engage infants in before they can talk, the more likely the infants will be to follow suit. This is modeling—pure and simple. Conversation must be modeled before it can be reproduced. Beyond that, the timing of language onset can be a big mystery, and reliance on averages can cause parents unnecessary anxiety if their child begins speaking later than might be expected. This anxiety can lead adults to behave in ways that seem to demand words ("Oh, you're hungry. Can you say 'milk'? Say 'milk'!").

Language and Social Learning (Pragmatics)

One of my earliest memories, enhanced by my grandmother's regular retelling, illustrates how demanding language of children backfires. My grandmother's best friend and coworker, Louise, had given me a wonderful Molly (Mrs. Davy) Crockett outfit, coonskin cap and all, which I just loved. It was decided that I would take a field trip to the elegant downtown boutique where they worked so I could say thank you. My mother drove me down to the store and my grandmother met me at the back door. She led me through the sewing room and dressing room area out to the showroom, where Louise was waiting. My grandmother said, "Ruth Anne, what would you like to say to Louise for giving you the Molly Crockett outfit?" Of course, I just stood there, lips buttoned up tightly. I expect I was prodded a few more times before my grandmother gave up in disgust. She gathered her coat and purse, and as she held my hand and walked me to where we would catch the bus home, I looked up at her and said, "I wouldn't say anything in there, would I?" My tiny but powerful grandmother's outrage was quickly tempered with amusement, and she always ended the story with, "I just wanted to pinch your little head off!"

This story helps me emotionally connect with tiny toddlers whose significant adults put pressure on them to speak before they are ready, whatever the context. When they are working so hard to make sense of the world and assign meaning to so many different words and phrases that are being spoken to them, I would rather honor them for the words they spontaneously produce than ask them to say specific words that make the adults feel good. *Please, thank you, I'm sorry, hello,* and *good-bye* are the most demanded words that parents feel they must hear. However, if toddlers are treated politely, if adults say please and thank you to them, they eventually understand the underlying emotions those words symbolize, and begin to use them naturally and appropriately.

Children learn the pragmatics of language just the same way they learn vocabulary and syntax—through modeling. Of course, when children reach the stage of language development in which they can say whatever they want, then some teaching of social appropriateness may be required. However, on-the-spot prompting ("What do you say...?") will always sound condescending and disrespectful to the "RIE ear." A private conversation about appropriate responses, which can perhaps be backed up by a secret glance the next time, will build more genuine respect into the child's nature.

I have had many parent–caregiver discussions about the imperious manner in which toddlers who have found their voices, so to speak, often demand service. Recently, a mother described how her daughter, Isadora, started her day shouting something like, "Get me some milk *now!*" From there, she would go on to more and more demands, making the morning getting-ready ritual a nightmare for the whole family. Knowing this family well, I concluded that Isadora was, indeed, working at the level of pragmatics, in which personal power is always an issue. She had the words, she had the grammar, but she was testing out a tone of voice that was inappropriate. It hurt her mother's feelings, made her father angry, and did not really get her what she wanted, quick service, because her mother and father did not want to reinforce her rude tone of voice by meeting her demands, even though what she wanted was actually what she needed, too.

It was my belief that Isadora's mistaken behavior was based on ignorance; she really did not understand the concept of rudeness, and that honey gets one more than vinegar. As her parents worked with her to help her learn more appropriate ways to ask for what she wanted, Isadora was engaged in refining her language, and ego, development to include pragmatically, and socially, appropriate ways of making her wants known. This fairly common toddler misstep does not usually last long if the adults in the child's life do not overreact or reinforce the undesired behavior. This is another example of the integrated nature of human development; it is impossible to completely tease apart the interface between language development and socialization, but using the RIE approach helps clarify all of the elements by responding to the child in an authentic manner. Isadora's mother began to say, "I know you are hungry, and I will get you some breakfast. But when you speak to me that way, it makes me not want to do things for you. Can you ask with a nicer voice?" Her father began to say, "It makes me angry when you yell at Mommy; it hurts my head," instead of yelling back. The emphasis on authenticity does not mean acting out of impulse, which can be harmful, but in letting the child know what one's feelings are so that she can make an informed adjustment. Adults so often make assumptions that young children can read them better than they really can. Yes, children are exquisitely emotionally attuned, but they are likely to misinterpret our behavior if we do not tell the child what is in our minds. Again, it is important that adults be intentional about *what* we are speaking, not just *that* we are speaking.

The Seeds of Literacy

Nowadays, it is considered essential to include literacy preparedness or preliteracy in the infant–toddler curriculum because literacy is such an important element of success in later academic and economic success

(Bowman, 2004). RIE offers a developmentally meaningful approach to the preliteracy dialogue, which I think has been frequently misinterpreted or misapplied. I was distressed to observe in a child care center in which I was going to be giving some training that 18–30-month-olds were being forced to sit in a circle for half an hour and repeat after their flash card-wielding teacher the names of letters, numbers, colors, and shapes ("Can you say 'ellipse'?"). What I learned from watching this was how

motivated (most) toddlers are to please the adults who have power over them, and how otherwise meaningless this activity was for them. I found myself inwardly rooting for the child who kept getting up to wander off to play, and being sad for him when he was reprimanded for doing what was actually the right thing. The teachers in this classroom were working really hard to do what they thought was right, but they were spending way too much energy controlling children who really just needed to play. Teachers and toddlers alike would be happier and more in harmony if literacy were seen as something adults demonstrated throughout the day ("I'm reading about how to make play dough.") and toddlers were allowed to freely and spontaneously join teachers for intimate moments reading books one on one or in small, lap-sized groups. If program directors feel teachers need to be more accountable, why not build into the routine an individual 10-minute, or less, reading time with each child, say after the morning diaper change? If the child learns to expect this, then when the child knows her diaper change is next, she can start picking out a book to read afterward. This can help to satisfy the parents that their child is getting adequate preliteracy experiences while enhancing the relationship with the caregiver (Honig, 2002). Parents can build on this by reading the book again with the child at the end of the day, allowing the child to share a very real part of his or her day with the parent, as a bridge between family and school.

A RIE-based approach to early or preliteracy for children under 3 would include a lot of respectful oral communication about things relevant to them, plenty of access to interesting books and adults to read them with, in a nondirective and curiosity-enhancing manner (Hammond, 2001). Nursery rhymes, songs, and the encouragement to play spontaneously with words ("Here is your soup for sipping! Sipping soup. Silly sipping soup!") are also wonderful ingredients for building language and relationships.

As children gain fine motor skills, a RIE-based program would also include access to age-appropriate writing utensils and paper, as well as the freedom to play at literacy tasks such as scribbling on notepads and "reading" on their own or with others. I have often been touched watching toddlers read to younger babies, or stuffed animals, because it so clearly shows how they have absorbed from their significant adults the joy of reading and the joy of togetherness. The idea of being able to read and write, and the inkling that there is meaning behind the mysterious symbols adults use, are what adults need to impart to infants and toddlers, but not at the expense of their freedom to actively explore and construct their knowledge of the real, three-dimensional world (Jones & Cooper, 2006).

Learning to express oneself is an important task of early childhood, and typically developing children will learn to do this without stress or effort when their adults talk with them in an authentic way, read with them in a relaxed atmosphere, and model both for the child to observe. Children with delays will also benefit from this approach along with whatever therapeutic interventions may be prescribed. Communication begets communication; effective self-expression is the natural outcome of solid relationships. The RIE approach to language and literacy cannot be separated from all of its other elements—trusting in the child's inner motivation is the key.

References

Bowman, B. (2004). Play in the multicultural world of children. In E. F. Zigler, D. G. Singer, & S. J. Bishop-Josef (Eds.), *Children's play: The roots of reading* (pp. 125–141). Washington, DC: ZERO TO THREE.

Gerber, M. (2002). *Dear parent: Caring for infants with respect* (expanded edition). Los Angeles: Resources for Infant Educarers.

Hall, E. T. (1976). *Beyond culture.* New York: Anchor Books/Doubleday.

Hammond, R. A. (2001). Preparing for literacy: Communication comes first. *Educaring, 22*(40), 1.

Hart, B., & Risley, T. R. (1995). *Meaningful differences in the everyday experience of young American children.* Baltimore: Brookes.

Honig, A. S. (2002). *Secure relationships: Nurturing infant/toddler attachment in early care settings.* Washington, DC: National Association for the Education of Young Children.

Jones, E., & Cooper, R. M. (2006). *Playing to get smart.* New York: Teachers College Press.

Lareau, A. (2003). *Unequal childhoods: Class, race and family life.* Berkeley: University of California Press.

Mangione, P. (1999). Recent research on language development. *Educaring, 20*(3), 1.

Meier, D. (2004). *The young child's memory for words: Developing first and second language and literacy.* New York: Teacher's College Press.

Schore, A. N. (1994). *Affect regulation and the origin of the self.* Hillsdale, NJ: Erlbaum.

Schore, A. N. (2003). *Affect disregulation and disorders of the self.* New York: W.W. Norton.

Yamamoto, K. (1993). *Their world, our world: Reflections on childhood.* Westport, CT: Praeger.

Chapter 5

Setting Limits That Make Sense

Culturally based attitudes toward freedom, of which one may not be consciously aware, influence adults' attitude about what limits should be placed upon a child's innate desire to explore and act on the world. The RIE approach generally upholds the notion that personal freedom is a human right that goes hand in hand with the obligation to respect the rights and needs of others (Hammond, 2001). The dual task, then, is to (a) promote infants' and toddlers' self-initiated activities while keeping them safe and (b) maintain one's own sense of order, sanity, and self-respect in the process. Setting behavioral limits and intervening respectfully is the key to creating a mutually rewarding attitude of give-and-take that ultimately leads to genuine cooperation. This chapter elaborates on how this looks in various situations and at different stages of infant–toddler development.

One of the important ways in which the RIE approach helps children develop a sense of security and trust in others and themselves is by promoting clear and consistent limits. Because RIE practitioners believe that children should be allowed to move and play freely whenever possible, there is sometimes a misperception that "RIE children" are allowed to do whatever they want. Of course, this is a ridiculous notion; no child could survive, let alone thrive, who was raised without constraints placed upon her impulses. Even when basic safety is maintained, allowing a child to believe there is no pressure to conform to appropriate social restraints sets them up for a sort of narcissism that does not promote healthy inner controls or relationships (Lieberman, 1993). All individuals must constrain themselves to maintain harmony in their families, workplaces, and other social settings. In that light, infants need adults' help from the beginning to build the foundation for self-control and respect of others.

Selective Intervention

What RIE offers to the whole area of child guidance is what Magda Gerber referred to as *selective intervention*. She promoted the concept of *red light, green light, yellow light* (Gerber, 2002). If the child is in a situation he can handle, the light is green and there is no need for intervention. If a child is about to breach an important safety or social rule, then the light is red and the adult intervenes: calmly, swiftly, unambiguously, and respectfully. Whether the issue is one of safety or social appropriateness, the adult does not moralize or shame, but simply explains why something is not safe or not okay, and, if necessary, uses a firm but kindly hand to prevent harm from occurring. Scolding is not ultimately useful in helping children internalize healthy inner controls (Sigsgaard, 2002). When there is a question as to whether the child is able to manage the situation on his own, this is symbolized by the yellow light. The adult comes close and observes to see what may be needed; there may be room for negotiation. These yellow light situations are more challenging for the adult; they require thinking on one's feet as well as patience. (See box, Selective Intervention, for examples of Red Light, Green Light, Yellow Light.)

A parent at the orientation for the infant–toddler program at Pacific Oaks once asked, "When should we start disciplining our toddler?" In my head, I thought, "Well, if you're just now asking, it's already too late," but of course I did not say that. What I did was ask the group, as Magda had regularly done, what the word *discipline* really means. In any group, there is always someone who says, "punishment," and I think the father in this story had this concept in mind when he asked his question. This question was often the jumping off place where Magda would begin to discuss her perspective on discipline, as in "disciple: a follower or pupil of a leader, teacher, philosophy, etc." (*Oxford Illustrated Dictionary*, 1998), wherein a person would want to conform him- or herself to the likeness of an admired other. The father was correct in presuming that punishment is inappropriate with infants; his question, I think, was really about when punishment can be utilized. Magda never advocated punishment as a deterrent; her ideas were much more subtle and presumed that the child's inner agenda included a desire to have the parent's approval.

Selective Intervention: Red Light, Green Light, Yellow Light

Situation 1: A newly walking toddler starts up a low ramp, just as another child begins to come down.

Green light: The adult observes without moving in because it is not likely to be serious if a child should tumble; it would be a learning experience. The two toddlers accommodate one another beautifully and continue on their way.

Red light: As the two children reach the middle of the ramp, one reaches up to grab a handful of the other's hair, to get him to move aside. The adult has been watching and now moves in quickly saying, "Oh, Ava, that is hurting Jadyn. Please let go of his hair," putting a gentle but deci-sive hand on Ava's, ready to help her let go if she does not stop.

Yellow light: The toddler at the top of the ramp deliberately blocks the other one's progress, looking like he might push. The ascending toddler looks over at the adult with a frightened face. The adult moves in quietly, saying to the upper toddler, "Keita wants to finish climbing up; can you let him by, Emmett? Then you can go down." Emmett responds readily to the supportive suggestion.

Situation 2: A baby crawls toward a neighbor's dog, and looks up at her mother with a questioning expression.

Green light: The mother knows the dog is good with small children and says, smiling, "Oh, Figo is coming. Do you want to touch his soft fur?" The baby pats the dog happily.

Red light: The mother does not know this dog, and moves in to pick up the baby until the dog's owner arrives.

Yellow light: It is just a puppy, and the mother sits down on the grass and keeps a hand ready to support both baby and puppy as she nar-rates their contact.

Situation 3: A toddler seems to be chewing something while playing. It is against classroom rules to eat except at the table. The adult approaches the child to see what he is mouthing.

Green light: It turns out just to be his tongue he is playing with. No inter-vention required!

Red light: The adult discovers that the child is mouthing a small ½-inch round magnet that must have rolled in from the adjacent prekinder-garten room. The adult says, "Please give me the magnet; it's not safe to have in your mouth." If the child does not give it up, the adult must then take more direct measures: "If you don't want to spit it out now,

continued

then I'm going to hold you until you are ready." The adult sits down with the child on her lap, presuming the toddler will be more motivated to let it go if his play is interrupted. (Forcibly extracting an object from a toddler's mouth might make him more likely to choke on or swallow it. Crying and struggling only increase the risk.)

Yellow light: The child has extracted a leftover piece of breakfast bagel from his pocket and is chewing a big wad while climbing the steps of the climbing structure. The adult says, "If you want to eat, I want you to sit down at a table until you're finished. If you want to play, I'll put the bagel in the trash." Either choice is acceptable to the adult.

Magda's first principle regarding discipline was that adults taking care of children had to be loving and display admirable qualities themselves to set the standard. She gave us no leeway to follow the "Do as I say, not as I do" approach. If adults want children to eat only healthy foods, they cannot get away with munching on chips while insisting that the child eat carrot sticks. In addition, how can adults manage children's temper tantrums if they are busy having their own? Adults need to be worthy role models of kindness and self-restraint to begin with, if the goal is to guide children toward greater self-discipline. Without apology, but with full recognition that there are other ways of guidance, RIE supports the development of inner self-discipline as the goal; it provides even very young children with the needed tools to self-regulate, which does include plenty of adult influence and authentic communication. An adult who is sensitive to the child's growing capacities will recognize that his or her own self-regulation is essential.

Having developmentally and individually appropriate expectations for a child is the next challenge. Starting with infancy, discipline is fairly simple. Adults usually do not think of it as discipline at all, as the father in the orientation exemplified. The first element of inner discipline is a kind of regularity of taking care of the self: eating when hungry, resting when tired, using effort in goal-oriented activities. A regular daily routine based on the baby's temperament and individual cyclical needs is the primary ingredient in starting an infant off with the necessary resources to become self-disciplined. (Setting up such care routines has already been discussed in chapter 8.)

Safety is also an important factor in the ultimate goal of self-discipline. When adults are engaged in setting limits for infants, it is easy to recognize that they cannot be expected to know much about how to keep themselves safe. Adults must mediate between their small explorers and the environment to make sure that safety is maintained and that hazards are eliminated until they are mature enough to recognize and avoid or appropriately manage them. As soon as they can begin to move around on their own, which can be as early as 3 or 4 months of age, the whole issue begins to get more complicated as adults must allow freedom and exploration in a safe yet challenging environment. There is further discussion of this in succeeding chapters 6 and 7.

A whole industry has emerged to help parents baby-proof their homes. (Of all the businesses profiting from parents' fears, it is the one that I would be least likely to challenge.) Electrical outlet covers, safety latches for cabinets and drawers, toilet seat locks, baby gates, and the like are important inventions that allow parents to relax a little. Also at this stage, it is essential to eliminate from the baby's environment not only the hazards but also the objects that may be safe but inappropriate. Better to put the DVDs and precious books out of reach than to get into a battle of wills. Better to gate off the areas of the home that are off limits, such as the kitchen and bathroom, than to be constantly saying, "No," and dragging the baby backward from the forbidden zone. It is better to let the environment set the limit than to be continually restricting and redirecting a baby whose very important job is to explore its new world. Having fascinating but forbidden objects or areas accessible to a baby is giving confusing messages and overtaxing her limited impulse control. This is the exact opposite of the RIE principle of setting clear and consistent limits (Gerber, 1979). Obviously, child care programs will hold themselves to a high standard for safety. Making the environment a partner is covered in chapter 3. Remembering Magda's image helps to set the bar: What if you were locked out for 4 hours? Even though they would certainly be emotionally distraught, would the children be physically safe until you returned?

In a nutshell, "discipline" during the infant stage consists of (a) building trust and affection between adult and child so that the child will want to please, (b) offering consistency in daily routines that support self-regulation, and (c) providing safe places in which a baby can follow his innate drive to explore without too much interference. If all of these measures are provided, the baby will reach toddlerhood—that is, Erikson's (1950) "autonomy stage"—with a secure enough foundation that the necessary constraints which so frustrate toddlers will be more tolerable to the child and therefore more easily maintained by the adult.

Keeping a baseline of order and peace in a home or classroom is essential if adults' goal is to rear children who carry an inner template of order and peace with them into their adult lives. This does not have to mean being overly concerned with messes or expecting toddlers to be quiet and low key. It does, however, mean that toddlers experience order as adults tidy up at various transition times and invite them to participate, and that adults use polite words and tones of voice when setting expectations for children's behavior.

If much of limit setting with toddlers has to do with safety, the rest has to do with helping them to be socially appropriate. This is really an issue of emotional safety in the long run. In either case, what toddlers need is twofold. They need information to help them build an accurate worldview ("We are meeting Katie and her family at the restaurant. You can draw on the placemats with Katie while we wait for our food."), and they need adequate supervision to make sure they do not overstep the bounds set for them ("I'd like you to keep your giggles quieter, please, so we do not bother the people in the next booth."). Magda was a big proponent of "I-messages" (Gordon, 1970) because they are an authentic and effective way to let children know when the adult is taking charge of a situation. It may take many repetitions of words and follow-through actions before a child has internalized a rule or guideline, and they will certainly test. Calm consistency is the key.

If an adult says, "I want you to get down off the table, please," but only takes action (and gets angry) on the fifth reminder, toddlers will generalize the lesson that the adult does not mean business until the fifth repetition she says anything. They will also come to expect adults to be angry at them. However, if the adult gets up as soon as she sees what is happening and walks calmly to where the child is climbing on the table, and says, "Please climb down; I want the table to stay clean for lunchtime," the child will get into the habit of believing the adult means business and perhaps even that the adult's requests are reasonable, whether they like them or not. Toddlers understand the meaning of an adult's physical presence; words do not yet have the same power. At this point, the adults are building toward the stage when their words or the recollection of their words will be sufficient, but the foundation for this is their willingness to take swift and appropriate action with toddlers.

When adults' simple proximity is not enough to scaffold appropriate behavior, they can still allow the child to exercise her personal power by offering a choice that will satisfy either way, such as, "Do you want to climb down by yourself, of shall I lift you off the table?" Often, this is all that is needed, and the toddler will climb down. However, if the child continues without acknowledging the request, it may be necessary to choose for her, saying, "It looks like you don't want to climb down, so I will take you off. I've already cleaned the table." Even limiting touches should be kind and gentle. This is the respectful approach; the adult has not acted on the child without offering an alternative. The adult may have thwarted an impulse, but will not have compromised her integrity; saving face is as meaningful to toddlers as it is to adults. However, if an adult is

feeling very angry and his hands are too tense while lifting t
down, troubles are likely to escalate.

When toddlers are in a testing mode, and openly defy a
tions, adults often feel they need some sort of recourse, ir
adequately communicate their displeasure. Some children are in
comply to avoid the adult's disapproval but others are not. A scowl or the
withdrawal of attention is a loud enough message for the easy-to-manage
toddler. More persistent negative behavior can be a way for a toddler to
signal distress on some level, and some quiet time alone with the adult
will often ease the stress. Sometimes, however, a little time alone, as a
chance to "reset" the nervous system, will help an older toddler get herself in hand. With some children, just changing the tone ("Let's rock in
the rocking chair for a few minutes and pretend you're my baby again,
OK?") can reboot the system, so to speak. In guiding children toward self-
discipline, it is all about how the adults support the child's ability to handle
emotional ups and downs through either self-calming auto-regulation or
cooperative co-regulation (Schore, 2003).

A mother who is at the end of her rope can grant herself some time
alone to do the same; this brief withdrawal of adult attention may also
have the desired affect on the toddler as well. The point is that a time
away is not retributive punishment; it is simply a chance to regroup and
model productive ways to de-stress. Toddlers may howl in protest, which
is their right, but when a change of pace is called for, it is healthier for the
child if adults follow through than if they allow unacceptable behavior to
persist. It is surprising how sunny a child's disposition can become after a
small battle of this sort. On some level, it seems children want, they even
need, to "lose" some battles. The loss of an inaccurate perception of the self
as the be-all and end-all is really a gain in the drive to become fully human.
It is, as described so beautifully by Judith Viorst (1986), a "necessary loss"
of the toddler rapprochement stage of the separation–individuation process
(Mahler, 1980).

As adults set limits on toddlers that make life run smoothly, they are
modeling for the toddlers the notion that one's self-respect can be maintained by not letting the world, or a feisty toddler, walk all over you. If
adults neglect this important function, from either over-empathy with the
child or simple laziness, adults deprive toddlers of the tools they will need
to fit comfortably and productively into society as they mature. My mother's
standard of discipline was that she wanted her children to be welcome
wherever they go. People who are pleasant to be around get more of the
"goodies" in life, so guiding children to become self-disciplined and socially
sensitive just makes sense.

A word about authenticity is in order here: Young children need to
have access to their parents' emotional range, in order to learn how to

identify and understand the world of emotion. Having a parent show you, through his genuine emotional response, what your affect is on another person provides an important element of social learning, so long as the parent does not unleash an unmanageable torrent of anger, rage, or grief on the child. Seeing true irritation, exasperation, or mild but real anger in response to inappropriate behavior is instructive. Nevertheless, adults' more negative emotions such as anger and frustration must be well-modulated to protect the child's formation of a healthy sense of self (Schore, 1994). The family bond creates a safe and reasonably forgiving place for a wide range of emotions. As the saying goes, "Love covers over a multitude of sins."

However, when adults are responsible for another family's child, they must maintain a certain professional distance and emotional neutrality. Relationships between young children and the professionals who care for them are by nature less profound than between parent and child, though still exceedingly important. The professional has more objectivity, if less passion, than the parent, which allows one to be more the master of one's emotional responses than a parent with her own child. Underlying trust and comfort can easily be lost if the adult breeches professionalism by showing too much emotion. Young children have enough to do to manage all of the various feelings flying around in a family; they do not need more to further complicate their lives. Yes, they deserve our attention and warmth and respect and insight, of course, but adults can do the most for them if they stay calm and "unhooked" when toddlers are having their own emotional upheavals. This does not mean a lack of empathy is required, but simply that professional boundaries are in place.

One last useful thought concerning discipline and some of the difficult feelings it brings out was expressed at a workshop for RIE Associates given by Emmi Pikler's daughter and current director of the Institute, Anna Tardos (1996). She said that it should always be the responsibility of the adult to start building the bridge back to harmony when there is a break in the synchrony (or attunement) between a child and adult. Making the child woo the adult back is too big a burden and smacks of emotional manipulation. When both adult and child are back in a more positive state of mind, an invitation from the adult to read a book or get a drink of water will signal to the child that relationships are reparable even when there have been disagreements. The repair is more powerful than the rupture of synchrony. Recovering from emotional dissonances is an essential skill adults must model by demonstration in order for children to fully flower.

The ongoing need to be fully present as a parent or caregiver, in prox-imity rather from across the room, often feels relentless, and sometimes emotionally exhausting. Yet when done with empathy and respect, it pays dividends in children who ultimately require less adult oversight because they have internalized reasonable guidelines for living. In other words, a fully present adult pays off in pleasant children who are welcome wherever they go.

References

Erikson, E. (1950). *Childhood and society.* New York: W.W. Norton & Co.

Gerber, M. (Ed.). (1979). *The RIE manual for parents and professionals.* Los Angeles: Resources for Infant Educarers.

Gerber, M. (2002). *Dear parent: Caring for infants with respect* (expanded edition). Los Angeles: Resources for Infant Educarers.

Gordon, T. (1970). *P. E. T.: Parent effectiveness training.* New York: Plume.

Hammond, R. A. (2001). Peaceful foundations. *Educaring, 22*(2), 3.

Lieberman, A. (1993). *The emotional life of the toddler.* New York: The Free Press.

Mahler, M. S. (1980). Rapprochement subphase of the separation–individuation process. In R. Lax, S. Bach, & J. A. Burland (Eds.), *Rapprochement: The critical subphase of separation–individuation* (pp. 3–19). New York: Jason Aronson.

Oxford illustrated dictionary. (1998). New York: Oxford University Press.

Schore, A. N. (1994). *Affect regulation and the origin of the self.* Hillsdale, NJ: Erlbaum.

Schore, A. N. (2003). *Affect regulation and the repair of the self.* New York: W.W. Norton & Co.

Sigsgaard, E. (2002). *Scolding: Why it hurts more than it helps.* New York: Teachers College Press.

Viorst, J. (1986). *Necessary losses: The loves, illusions, dependencies and impossible expectations that all of us have to give up in order to grow.* New York: Fawcett Gold Medal.

Part II

Initiative, Integrity, and Autonomy

Chapter 6

Freedom of Movement and Self-Awareness

At the same time that an infant is learning about herself while being spoken to, caressed, and handled by adults, she is also learning about how to operate her own body, how it moves, what she can cause it to do, and how to live peacefully within it. If respectful interactions during care are the first way she learns about her body and its various parts, the other equally important aspect of learning on the physical level is autonomous movement. The seminal research on natural movement development, done over many years by Emmi Pikler with the infants at The Pikler Institute, shows that typically developing infants do not need to be taught how to crawl, sit, stand, or walk. These milestones are only a few of the rewarding and fascinating physical skills infants who are allowed to move freely show us. Giving infants, even if they have developmental delays, the freedom to move in accordance with their innate impulses may seem radical, but it is essential to their becoming persons with uncompromised self-esteem. In this chapter, I discuss what is required from adults and the environment to ensure infants and toddlers the benefits of free movement.

The RIE approach to gross motor—or psychomotor—development is very easy to sum up with Magda Gerber's caveat, "Never put a baby into a position she cannot get into or out of all by herself"

(M. Gerber, personal communication, November, 1986). It sounds simple enough, but it actually challenges many assumptions that people have about babies, and makes adults question some of their basic coping strategies.

This applies first to how adults hold a young baby. The cultural norm here in the United States is to get them vertical as soon as possible without ever even thinking about it. Just about everyone I know holds babies upright against their shoulders. However, in The Pikler Institute, and in some RIE homes and centers, infants are transported in the arms with the head and spine fully supported in a supine or mildly tilted position until the baby has learned to sit up on her own, usually not before 6, 7, or more months of age.

Only when the baby has demonstrated that his musculoskeletal infrastructure is strong enough to fully support his head atop a straight back is the baby carried in an upright position. These babies are allowed to develop a deep sense of bodily security; they are not asked to struggle to hold up their heads with muscles that are unfit for the job. Making a baby wobble and strain to stay upright is not a good use of his energy and effort. When a body is required to do compensating work, movement habit patterns are formed that may cause other problems and compensations down the road that may then seem inexplicable. Allowing infants to develop their movements naturally and in sequence, without rushing past interim stages, provides them with a solid psychomotor foundation, which will support them for life. Infants have not yet divorced the mental from the physical senses of self, and if adults are careful, perhaps infants will always remain wholly integrated.

I have to admit that when my children were babies, I held them upright, too, and they really were only supine for breast-feeding. They would fuss and cry when held flat if no breast was offered because of this association. However, when a baby is always carried in a supine position, this expectation does not result. As Magda often said, babies come to expect and "need" whatever they become used to, whether it is the best thing for them or not.

The inner drive to be upright is hard to turn off once it has been turned on, but when babies are allowed to "hang out" on their backs until they can do otherwise without help, eventually they can do so many things through their own initiative that they love being on the floor to play. They look like little Martha Graham dancers with incredible grace and balance as they move through many transitional positions on their way to genuine upright posture.

While discussing the benefits of supine carrying in one of my RIE classes, a new mother said, "Well, that makes sense, but Everett [3½ months] has the tendency to squirm all over the place, getting himself in a lot of positions and straightening his legs to where he is almost standing, and I can't keep him in one position!" I said to her that her "dance" with Everett would be theirs alone, and that her response to his movements is really important; the mutual subtle and not-so-subtle adjustments that are made—body to body—are an important source of sensory stimulation that contributes to well-rounded brain development and sense of self and other. This is why I would rather see a baby being carried in the arms than in an infant carrier, where the baby conforms to one static lifeless shape for long periods of time. I cannot imagine that the bilateral development of the body–brain connection is nearly as complex in babies who spend long periods of their days strapped in infant seats, swings, or other inhibiting devices. In group care, of course, infants do not spend much time in adults' arms, because of the adults' responsibility for multiple children, which is why the stimulation of autonomous movement during noncare waking hours is so important.

In peaceful periods between feedings, diaperings, other care activities, and naps, most new babies enjoy being placed on their backs on a blanket or a lambskin in nonbinding clothing—or none if weather permits. In this position they have the maximum opportunity to move their arms and legs freely, to learn that they have control over them, and, ultimately, to discover their hands (Roche, 1994). Placing a baby gym with hanging toys over infants discourages them from trying to roll over, which is the gateway to many important learning opportunities. Watch a baby not under a gym patiently stretch and strain to reach a nearby toy of her own choosing. You will see an actively involved person who is developing not only muscles and skills, but also a willingness to work hard. And she will probably surprise herself one day as she stretches across her body for a toy and rolls over.

Another mistaken assumption is that babies benefit from being put on their tummies from the earliest weeks. There is no reason to place a typically developing baby on its tummy. When they are ready to be on their tummies, after having been given plenty of "back time" on a firm surface, they  will eventually flip over on their own. Babies who are not being restrained into back-lying or propped positions in infant seats, carriers, or the like— but who are given freedom to lie on their backs on a firm, flat surface in an adequate amount of space—will spend the right amount of time, for them, playing on their backs. From here, they will begin rolling to the side, back and forth, until they turn over, and then it is just a matter of time until they are administering "tummy time" for themselves. Any flattening of the head, which seems to be a new worry for parents, will be minimal and temporary. Furthermore, compensatory efforts will not set off a cascade of less-than-ideal muscular habits. If pediatricians would encourage plenty of "floor time" for free movement rather than tummy time, there would be more awareness that babies come with their own bodily intelligence and time tables—as well as more happy, active babies, too.

In two of my RIE parent–infant classes recently, there were babies (one boy, one girl) in each class who were making the parents anxious by not rolling onto their tummies after all of the other babies had. These two infants were both perfectly happy on their backs, and they found many ways to play in that position. Each was almost 10 months by the time they rolled over. What was fascinating was that they both not only rolled over in class for the first time, but also actually pushed up onto their elbows, raising their chests off the mat seemingly effortlessly. They easily held their heads up, looking around with pleasure and a bit of surprise—and for 20 minutes! These babies were truly ready to be on their tummies. (I wish developmentalists everywhere were as concerned about readiness in movement as they are about readiness in literacy.) It should be noted that neither suffers from persistent plagiocephaly, flat heads, after all that time on their backs because they were unrestrained. The little girl did have a touch of minor flattening, but it went away very quickly on its own. Her father, a young pediatrician, will not be telling the parents in his practice to impose tummy time on their infants. (See box Try Tummy Time Yourself for more information on tummy time.)

Recently a mother in a RIE parent–infant class asked me what to do when her baby, Ava, kept rolling onto her tummy and crying to be turned back over. I reassured her that Ava was doing just what she needed to do because by practicing her new skill she will build the neural pathways, procedural memory, to make turning over something she will be able to do gracefully without even thinking about it. She and I were, at that moment, watching Ava turn to her tummy and lift her head to look at the other babies lying near her on the mat. As she got tired, she started to fuss. I told her mother that it is sometimes necessary to delay an intervention, to allow a little time for the baby to struggle so that the next skill can emerge (although one should not delay the intervention to the point at which the infant is crying outright). So she and I tried it right there. Before our eyes, Ava developed the next skill she needed—how to rest comfortably until she had the energy again to resume her interaction with her environment. What she did was pull her knees in under her, turn her head to the side, grab a handful of the sheet covering the mat and pull it to her mouth, adding her tiny thumb for good measure. Then, she grinned

Try Tummy Time Yourself

Pretend you are a baby and you do not yet have the strength or skill to use your arms to help in lifting your heavy head, which you should imagine weighs twice as much as it actually does because proportionally, this is true for babies. Now lift just your head and see how long it is comfortable to hold it up. How does your neck feel? Your shoulders? Also, what can you see with both eyes? Can you see both of your hands? What is the range of motion of your arms and legs, lying flat on your tummy and unable to raise your shoulders? Take your time. Now gently turn yourself over and see what it is like to be on your back. How does your breathing feel? What is the potential range of motion of your arms and legs in this position? Can you engage your abdominals to lift your legs in the air? What can you see by moving your head around? Can you see both hands at once? Could you stay here awhile comfortably? Where could you possibly go from here? Now... what do you think of tummy time?

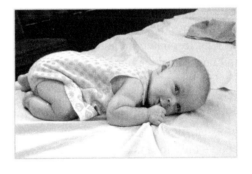

up at me, eyes twinkling, thumb and cloth still in her mouth. She stayed there for another 10 or 15 minutes. Her mother remarked that it was the longest time she had spent on her tummy, ever. Of course, the stimulation of being with the other babies, as well as the peaceful atmosphere of the outdoor, tree-shaded deck of the RIE house, contributed to her pleasure. (This inspired a further conversation as to how to give Ava more such outdoor experiences in spite of living in an apartment with no yard. Jean, the mother, came up with the idea of taking a mat or blanket to the park to lay her on the grass under a tree, which sounded perfect.)

The next assumption that needs to be looked at is the notion that babies need to be sat up so they can use their hands. In fact, floor-bound but mobile babies use their hands and feet to play with objects all of the time. Sitting babies up before they can get there on their own causes undue strain on the hips and groin, an unhealthy curve of the back and compression of the lungs caused by slumping. This positioning creates a situation in which the baby cannot go toward what he wants; the adult must bring the toys to him. He is likely to fall over if he reaches beyond the end of his arm, and so he calls for help. Being placed in a sitting position stops him from doing what he can do (move around on the floor), causes him to have to do what he cannot safely do (try to balance without falling over), and requires that he get help he would not otherwise need (to get the toys that roll away). Sitting a baby up before he can get in or out of the position on his own teaches a baby to be helpless (Gerber, 1989) and may contribute to a habit of physical insecurity, which may in turn affect his underlying self-confidence. In addition, this positioning sometimes results in a baby who is weak and somewhat immobilized in the pelvic region, possibly skipping crawling altogether, thus missing the important cross-lateral movement that is so important in overall brain development (Hannaford, 2005). Babies who have been sat up sometimes learn to locomote in a sitting position by using their hands to scoot on their bottoms, which gets them places, but does not activate the brain in a cross-lateral way. It also causes immobility in the pelvic region with crawling and walking being further impaired. This is not a naturally occurring stage (Pinto & Money, 2006).

It has been my experience that some babies who are routinely sat up develop an aversion to being on their backs, and cry when placed this way on the floor. As Magda always pointed out, babies are creatures of habit and learn to prefer what they are used to, whether it is good for them or not. It is common that these babies never learn to crawl, but go straight to pulling up and walking, without having a chance to gain all of the benefits of crawling. These are often the same babies who are "helped" to walk as their hands are held over their heads. They can get very hooked on this activity as well. The parents are then called upon to "walk" the baby wherever she wants to go, and there can be a backlash of exhaustion on the part of the parents when they tire of being the child's only means of exploration. Walking is a skill that requires the ability to balance on one foot at a time, and if adults are holding their hands, they do not gradually acquire this skill as they strengthen the necessary joints and muscles (Gerber, 1989). Fortunately, babies are capable of learning a new habit—one of self-sufficiency and self-confidence—when the parents or caregivers are willing to allow the child to express her frustration (yes, that may mean some crying in complaint) as they gently but with conviction encourage her to try new ways of reaching her goals.

Babies who are put in walkers and other exercise contraptions actually tend to be delayed in their acquisition of the skill (Garrett, McElroy, & Staines, 2002). Crawling is the best preparation for walking, and babies who have learned to walk as their hands were held do not place their weight on their feet in the biomechanically correct way, often walking on the outsides of their feet. Another down side of handheld walking is that when infants do begin to walk on their own, they tend to reach up for rescue when they fall, rather than reaching down to break their fall. The bottom line is that a baby needs to develop his own relationship gravity. As Magda so elegantly said, "Learning to fall, getting up moving on is the best preparation for life" (Gerber, 1989). She also out that infants who are in charge of their own movement in an a ate environment develop good judgment about what they can and ...ot safely do.

As infants become toddlers, they start to take more risks. An adult's attitude toward their explorations has a big impact on their sense of competence and self-confidence. The habit of telling young explorers "You're OK" if they have an upsetting mishap does not provide the information (never mind empathy) to help them understand what just happened. For instance, as 2-year-old Liam begins to wail from an unexpected trip over a rock, his mother, Gabby, comes close and calmly says, "You tripped on the rock. That was a big surprise. Are you OK?" She waits as Liam takes inventory of his body and begins to stand back up, still crying. At this point, Gabby says, "Did that hurt? Do you want a hug?" He moves into her arms and snuggles in for some comfort. In addition to the experience of being understood, he has heard a number of words. Chances are the word *tripped* will mean something to him from now on, and maybe *surprise* will have a more nuanced definition. He will also have added to his sense of agency, the recognition that his own action caused the mishap, not the rock. By neither over-empathizing, which teaches them to be fearful, nor under-empathizing and expecting them to be tough, adults are able to allow children to make their own determination as to the seriousness of the event, and seek comfort if it is needed, or move on if it is not.

This circumspect approach to a mishap may seem a little cold and unfeeling to some, but the important thing is not our feelings, but the child's. Observing in order to be in synchrony with the child's feelings, rather than letting our feelings be primary in the interaction, gives the child the opportunity to become self-aware (Gonzalez-Mena & Eyer, 2008). Children may sometimes need to be told how to *behave*, but if adults want them to learn to trust their own experience, it would be unwise to tell them how to *feel*. Allowing infants and toddlers to connect with their own inner experience, especially concerning their own bodies, sets the tone for mutually respectful relationships. Children are more likely to communicate freely when they believe their internal evaluations will be respected. An open mind and heart is the underlying invitation to a trusting relationship.

In an article I wrote for RIE's newsletter, *Educaring* (Hammond, 1999), called "Why Hovering Isn't Helpful," I describe a little boy who just walks off of steps because he is used to having someone always there to catch him. This is something toddlers who have been reared with RIE principles in mind almost never do because they are attentive to their own whereabouts. Also, a child who is put somewhere will not know what it will take to get down safely. As my friend and colleague Deborah Greenwald says, "If you drive somewhere, you know where you are. If you are a passenger getting there, you may have no idea how to get home." The same goes for climbing. The joy and sense of empowerment they express after they have mastered a challenging climb is equal to explorer Sir Edmund Hillary's triumphant climb up Mount Everest.

The RIE approach to observation shares much with the dance movement therapy principle that "each of us has a need and a desire to be seen and understood for who we really are—to be witnessed without prejudice" (Tortora, 2006, p. 65). This is why all RIE parent–infant classes include a period of quietly focused observation of the infants and toddlers during free play. Our attention, without distraction, comment, or judgments tells them by our actions that we appreciate them, that we value their activity, and that we want to know them for who they are. This kind of attention builds richly nuanced attachment when coupled with regular attentive, responsive caregiving.

Trusting infants and toddlers to be in charge of their own movement development may seem radical. It certainly flouts the general perception of babies as helpless creatures who need adults to do everything for them. However, being trusted in this way sets the tone for mutually respectful communications down the road. With this in mind, it becomes a pleasure to observe the most obvious and measurable evidence of self-actualization taking place right before our eyes. As Magda always said, no one will ask on a job interview, "At what age did you learn to walk?"

References

Garrett, M., McElroy, A. M., & Staines, A. (2002). Locomotor milestones and babywalkers: Cross sectional study. *BMJ, 324* (7352), 1494. Retrieved July 27, 2009, from www.bmj.com/cgi/content/full/324/7352/1494?view = full&pmid = 12077035

Gerber, M. (1989). *See how they move* [Video/DVD]. Los Angeles: Resources for Infant Educarers.

Gonzalez-Mena, J., & Eyer, D. W. (2008). *Infants, toddlers, and caregivers.* New York: McGraw-Hill.

Hammond, R. A. (1999) Why hovering isn't helpful. *Educaring, 20*(3), 2.

Hannaford, C. (2005). *Smart moves: Why learning is not all in your head* (2nd ed.). Salt Lake City, UT: Great River Books.

Pikler, E. (1994). Peaceful babies—Contented mothers. *Sensory Awareness Foundation Bulletin, 14,* 5–24.

Pinto, C., & Money, R. (Eds.). (2006). *Unfolding of infants' natural gross motor development.* Los Angeles: Resources for Infant Educarers.

Roche, M. A. (Ed.). (1994). Emmi Pikler 1902–1984 [Special issue]. *Sensory Awareness Foundation Bulletin, 14.*

Tortora, S. (2006). *The dancing dialogue: Using the communicative power of movement with young children.* Baltimore: Brookes.

Chapter 7

Play as an Expression of Personhood

Watching infants at play is truly a pleasure and a privilege that RIE bestows upon its adherents. Observing infants and toddlers while they are engrossed in making new discoveries and consolidating their learning inspires respect for their innate competence and their commitment to their own education. If infants and toddlers are allowed plenty of uninterrupted time for play in an environment that includes peers and a variety of objects with different qualities to explore (toys is too limiting a term), they will have the real-life, hands-on knowledge of the world that is the foundation for later academic education (Jones & Cooper, 2005). By paying attention to their play without overpowering them with our own ideas, we may get a glimpse of how infants view the world (Hammond, 2007). This aspect of the RIE approach is one that liberates adults to relax and enjoy being with children without worrying that they should be constantly teaching them. This chapter includes vignettes that elucidate the purpose and meaning of independent and social play in the development of intelligent and thoughtful children.

In her classes, after everyone had brainstormed the question, "What is play?" Magda Gerber always, in my experience, capped the session with the statement, "Play is for play's sake only." It has taken me a long time to really appreciate her point, but I think I am finally understanding.

I think she meant that whenever someone else's agenda gets inserted into another person's play, it has ceased to be pure play, and has become something else. Her statement was, in a sense, a warning that if adults decide to teach by inserting their own "curriculum" into an infant's play, they may be tampering with an essential tool in the child's educational process, namely, his self-generated and self-renewing curiosity and joy of discovery. There used to be this little framed quotation from Jean Piaget up on the wall in the RIE house: "Whenever we teach a child something, we forever destroy his chance to discover it for himself." Or, as Magda paraphrased, "Be careful what you try to teach; you may be interfering with what the baby is learning." With so very many things to learn, why do we adults so often imagine that we know better than the babies themselves what they need to know sooner rather than later, and how much time it should take them to learn it? With just a little faith in their good sense, adults can relax and enjoy watching what babies want to do. Of course, adults provide the environment for them and offer them things to manipulate and discover; some are toys, some are everyday objects.

Adults can let babies know by our appreciative attention that their experiments are valued. If they invite us into their game, respectful adults are careful to let them be the leader and do not assume that our ideas have more value than theirs. It is easy to override an infant's self-confidence, and the RIE approach takes care to preserve their enthusiasm by respecting their ideas.

RIE practitioners maintain that play is what babies do when they are not involved in a caregiving activity or sleeping. The RIE-influenced adult has the expectation that a well-nurtured, rested, healthy baby will find a way to play without an adult having to elicit it. RIE parents often talk about the incredible relief involved in finding out that they do not have to be in charge of every minute of their baby's waking life and development. Professional caregivers who have RIE experience trust the babies in their groups to play while they are caring for the other babies.

Of course, infants need constant oversight, and they need to have their play supported by adults (Jones & Reynolds, 1992; Kálló & Balog, 2005) but they do not need perpetual interaction. They need times together with their adult(s), and they need times when they can be on their own, to find out about themselves as separate individuals and what their environment has to offer. Of course, they do love and need the playful attention of their parents and educarers, but it sets everyone up for frustration if babies get the idea that they must have an adult stimulating them all of the time. They get this idea when adults actually are stimulating them all of the time by talking, jiggling, rocking, swinging, moving them about, telling them what to look at, and so forth. We make life easier for everyone, however, by helping infants achieve a balance between the co-regulation offered by sensitive interactions with adults, and the self-regulation that autonomous play introduces. The RIE approach is not about pushing early independence but about allowing it to emerge. Of course, the role of temperament will play a part in how much time together and time apart babies prefer, but even babies who might be inclined always to be in interaction will benefit from some unmediated time with themselves.

For those with an appreciation of Erik Erikson's (1950) psychosocial stages of development, and who consider the idea that trust versus mistrust is the only dialectic of importance in the earliest months of life, a brief mention of Joan Erikson's (1988) perspective in *Wisdom and the Senses* may be helpful. Her idea is that the stages are present at all ages as potentialities and possibilities, but that as the life span plays out, each theme comes into sharper focus during certain times. When looked at in this light, it is clear that the RIE approach accounts for the development not only of trust in the first year, but also of autonomy and initiative (Kovach & Da Ros-Voseles, 2008), which are described in Erikson's Stages II and III, respectively. Also, the groundwork for intimacy (Erikson's Stage VI) is certainly being laid at this time as the relationships between babies and sensitive caregivers clearly show.

Another factor that must not be overlooked when thinking about the role of the adult in children's play, especially when the children are infants, is how cultural values are passed down from one generation to the next (Rogoff, 2003). Autonomy may not be on every family's Top 5 list of essential values. It should not be swept under the rug that a baby who is allowed to move and play freely from the beginning is likely to develop into a child who continues to expect to exercise a considerable amount of choice on his or her own behalf. Imagine my surprise after saying lovingly to my newly verbal toddler, "Are you Mommy's girl?" when she replied, "No, I'm my own girl!" As Magda used to say so unapologetically, "RIE is not for everyone." If this sort of self-ownership is not appreciated, then RIE principles may not support a family's desired results. It is RIE's bias, culturally speaking, to view infants as individuals with a right to age-appropriate autonomy, especially with regard to play. This does not mean that the child will automatically be selfish or uncooperative, not at all. It just means that she may be less inclined to suppress personal wants when issues come up for negotiation between family members or friends.

Whatever the culture, it is now widely appreciated among early childhood theorists that children learn through active play (Piaget, 1964; Zigler, Singer, & Bishop-Josef, 2004). This is as true for infants as for preschoolers. Magda's caveat that passive toys make active children and active toys make passive children calls for a distinction between play and entertainment. The dictionary defines entertainment as "amusement" (*New Oxford*

Dictionary of English, 1998). Of course, amusement is something people all want and need, but it can be either superficial or profound. If adults want infants to become deeply engaged, creative, and productive people, we need to help them become active constructors of rewarding experiences, not habitual consumers of entertainment. So, how do we do this?

Newborn to 3 Months

As stated in the previous chapter, newborns need freedom of movement at different times during the day when they are in a quiet–alert state, either in their cribs, a playpen, or on a mat in a cozy and safe place. They do not usually like wide open spaces, probably because they cannot see so far yet, and a few minutes in such a space may be all they want at first. Until babies have really learned to use their hands, toys are not of much use. After the baby has had the chance to gain some deliberate control, then is the time to place a few soft, lightweight objects near the baby, which she may grasp at first by accident. As babies learn and develop, they enjoy longer and longer free-play periods. In the life of an infant, as you can see, movement and play are often synonymous. Even though I have divided them into separate chapters, it is impossible to talk about one without crossing over into the other.

An assumption people make that impacts a baby's development is the belief that babies fuss because they are bored. This belief causes the adults to perform many interventions to entertain, while actually contributing to the need for more interventions. A baby who is used to constantly being bounced, jiggled, moved around, repositioned, or fussed over learns to expect this type of stimulation. All of this intervention does not give him the chance to develop the motivation to seek other types of stimulation over which he might have control. Of course face-to-face, loving, and joyful interactions with parents and significant others are absolutely essential to a baby's healthy development, but a chance to recognize one's own body parts, motivations, and interests also help him to contextualize himself. By putting him down, even for a few minutes while in a quiet–alert state, adults offer the baby the opportunity to find himself. Yes, he is part of a family, but he is, from the beginning, also his own unique self. This may be the biggest area in which the RIE approach distinguishes itself from other belief systems about babies.

Often people do things without realizing they inhibit development, such as placing toys in babies' hands when they are too young to let go because of the grasp reflex (White, 1975) or putting a baby gym structure with hanging toys over the baby, which gives her something to look at and bat at, but provides few truly satisfying activities (chewing, tasting,

dropping, picking up, banging, waving, etc.). Hand regard is a
activity for a young baby because it is an important precursor
all later hand–eye coordination. The joy of discovering our o
and that they can do our bidding, is a fascinating process when ...
is allowed (Pikler, 1969). If toys are hanging in your face, it is difficult to
focus on or even find your own hands in all of that visual chaos.

Placing toys around the baby where they can be accidentally or deliberately found and picked up, and accidentally or deliberately dropped and
rediscovered, provides a better inspiration for self-initiated movement and
the beginnings of play and fine motor development. Hanging mobiles are
another entertainment device that inhibits autonomous multisensory play,
especially at first. When babies are very young, they have a gazing reflex
over which they have little control (White, 1975). Therefore, just because
a baby is staring at a mobile does not mean the baby likes it or is benefit-
ing from the stimulation. It may just mean that her gaze has been
captured and she cannot look away. The more rewarding and beneficial
opportunity at this stage is to be able to see one's own hands and learn
how to move them in a chosen direction and how to open and close the
fingers at will. Only when this has been accomplished are toys useful.
While this is being learned, a wonderful object to place near a baby is a
simple cotton table napkin. Lay it flat, then pick up the center and lift it
into a peak. The baby may accidentally, at first, grasp the fabric, but
because it is porous and soft, it will not hurt if the baby covers her face or
cannot quite let go at will. You may see some early, self-initiated peekaboo
emerge as the baby moves into the next stage (Kálló & Balog, 2005).

Three to 6 Months

First toys for babies who have learned to grasp, in addition to the napkin, are O-balls, short chains of linking rings, small wooden bowls,
stainless condiment cups, small rag dolls or sock animals, and flexible sili-
cone coasters and muffin cups. A favorite toy of RIE babies is a partially
inflated beach ball so that it is big but soft enough for tiny fingers to
grasp. They seem to love being able to manipulate something that large. If
it is see-through, so much the better. (I feel like I am giving away highly
valuable trade secrets!)

The idea is to offer simple but varied objects with different shapes,
colors, materials, textures, and weights—but not all in one. My pet peeve,
with regard to baby toys, is when the designers try to pack as many variables into one toy as they can. Babies do not need the whole rainbow and
every possible shape and texture all in one toy. This is too confusing
and not conducive to the type of scientific inquiry that builds useful

knowledge. At this young age, they are looking at edges, feeling curves versus straight lines, fingering and licking textures, testing relative weights. As they learn that metal feels cooler than wood, cloth drapes but most kinds of plastic do not, or red is a discrete attribute and blue is another, they will eventually build their knowledge of the properties of matter so that when they are combined they are more comprehensible. When the objects presented to them are overly complex, this process is actually interfered with. One father and I had a fun and fascinating observation in class of Sophie, who was around 11 months old, licking first the wooden bench and then a shiny metal bowl, over and over, obviously contrasting and internalizing the sensory attributes of the two materials. We were glad there were no splinters!

A few notes about safety—besides the caveat to keep the play area free of items small enough to choke on—are in order. Because the baby primarily will be, for a number of weeks or even months, lying on its back holding objects above its face, the objects should not be heavy enough to hurt if dropped. My colleagues and I have eliminated many of what used to be our favorite "RIE toys" because of concerns over the safety of the ingredients in the plastic, such as the old suction-type soap holders. Much as the babies enjoyed them, they have been retired. (We are always on the lookout for safe new options, and kitchen stores are a fun place to search.)

The best way to respect an infant's readiness for a toy is to place it within his reach—or maybe even a tiny bit beyond—and allow the baby all of the time he needs to choose when to take notice. At most, if I am very eager for the toy to be discovered, I will hold the object in the baby's sight, but not shake it in his face, and let him track it as I place it nearby. If he is interested he will take the initiative.

As babies integrate gross motor progress with fine motor exploration, it is so fun to watch as they manipulate objects with two hands while lying on their sides, or even on their tummies, once they have lifted themselves

onto their elbows. The desire to use their hands is a great motivator for balancing in more and more precarious poses in the stages between rolling over and sitting up. There is no need to think that a baby needs to be sitting up to use both hands and practice hand–eye coordination.

Crawling

By the time a baby has progressed from rolling, a form that often comes first, to the forward locomotion of belly creeping on hands and knees, which comes before discoveri..., position when infants have not been propped to sit, balls of all types become even more fascinating. The same toys they have explored earlier now get used in different ways: The little stainless cups may become "hooves" as they crawl with one in each hand, making delightful clomping sounds. Baskets may be discovered as excellent places to put things. Hair curlers may be discovered to nest quite neatly (except they fall through!). Boxes become push toys as crawling evolves into knee walking. Peekaboo with scarves may now involve covering other toys up and revealing them at will. Low wooden platforms, ramps, and stair arches provide not only gross motor opportunities, but also hard surfaces against which to bang, roll, or push things. Cardboard boxes can be great places to creep into. (Masking tape on cut edges will eliminate paper cuts and scrapes.) Inflatable swimming pools with squishable sides—with or without water—make interesting terrain. All sizes, weights, and textures of balls motivate a lot of locomotion. (See box Coming Together at RIE for a description of what babies love about RIE class.)

Coming Together at RIE

Of course, the presence of other babies makes everything more interesting. The first self-initiated contact between two floor-bound babies on a mat is momentous, as hands clasp a responding other. Sometimes they will lie or sit and gaze deeply into one another's eyes and the depth of connection is breathtaking. The social connection with peers grows as they become mobile. They are fascinated to see what other babies are doing, and they take their time to really get to know one another. Their first conversations with parents often include the names of the other toddlers. Parents in RIE classes often remark that their 8- or 9-month-old starts excitedly squirming and squawking when he or she gets out of the car and realizes RIE class is the destination. Ninety minutes of unrestricted access to (a) parents' undivided attention, (b) interesting objects and equipment, (c) other babies, (d) freedom, and (e) bananas (I almost forgot!) make for a truly rich and rewarding experience, blending the physical, the cognitive, and the emotional in perfect harmony.

Toddlers

As crawlers become walkers, many new possibilities open up. They can reach door handles and higher shelves, and squeeze into narrow places. Thus, new approaches to safety are in order. New objects and pieces of equipment that hold a lot of meaning for the newly upright or those trying to become upright are (a) vehicles of all kinds in various sizes (It is shocking how early "vroom, vroom" enters the vocabulary!); (b) diverse baby dolls and other human representations (my RIE classes love these little linking plastic people we have); (c) carrying vessels with handles, which allow for collecting things and practicing balance simultaneously; and (d) kitchenware of all sorts, including empty plastic bottles of all sizes from 8-ounce water bottles to 5-gallon jugs. Those big jugs are great to push all around, to put things into, and to test one's strength. One of my little guys, Everett, who had gotten very good at walking, was testing himself by carrying a 3-gallon water jug up the stair climber, standing for a moment on the platform at the top of the three steps, and pushing the jug full of hair curlers down the steps. He stood there for a moment, grinning with pride at his accomplishment, needing to share his joy with the adults in the room, and then crawled down after it. While he repeated this activity at least eight times, in one form or another, his buddy, Avo, was testing his balance while sitting in a large round plastic tub reaching for balls and trying not to tip over. I always set up the environment with things other children at their stage have enjoyed, but I never know what they will do with it until they show me.

One day when my daughter was a young toddler I had read in some parents' magazine that, at her age, she should be able to stack 11 blocks into a tower. "Eleven?! Gee, I've never seen her stack blocks at all!" So, in a moment of non-RIE panic, I thought I had better see if she was capable of such a feat. I lured her into her room and got out the Duplo blocks. I began to model stacking the blocks, but she had something else in mind. She dumped out the whole bucket of blocks and began to scoot them across the wooden floor, using her little feet like a dust mop, until they bounced off the closet door, all the while making a raucous yet delightful sort of waterfall sound as she laughed with glee. What did I expect? She was a RIE-bred baby from Day One, with her own good ideas. I did not try testing her again.

Outdoor Play

It is impossible to address play for the older toddler without discussing the importance of being outdoors for part of each day. However, this is just as true for infants and younger toddlers, too. There is more and more evidence that being outdoors and being in nature lower stress and promote a sense of well-being. Young babies love to lay on a blanket and look up at trees, to feel the breeze come and go, to hear the  birds sing. Mobile infants are fascinated by the smallest details of nature, examining blades of grass or tasting bits of dirt with rapt attention (Ruebush, 2009). Toddlers on a half-hour walk that goes no further than the end of the driveway are attuning deeply to their world at a pace that allows them to gain understanding of the parts that make the whole. This leaf feels this way; rain makes puddles; rocks are heavy; the fence post is sunk into the ground. Taking a "walk" in a stroller is a walk for the adult, but the baby or toddler can only see as things go past. They do not get to touch, test, or taste anything except the snack or toys they have been given to pacify them while the adult gets exercise. It is okay to use a stroller this way, to a limited extent, because parents have needs, too, but it should not be thought of as a rich experience for the child. When toddlers can get out of the stroller or carrier, and get on the ground, with freedom to explore, then it becomes their walk.

In equipping a yard, whether it is at home or in a children's center, making the outdoors as accessible to the child as possible will lighten the load of the parent or caregiver. Being cooped up inside is not any child's idea of a great day. I know firsthand that residents of Southern California are spoiled; it is easy to have free flow from indoors to outdoors here, and children can go barefoot almost all year. Yet even in harsher climates, children are done a disservice if they are denied their rightful place in nature. Richard Louv (2005), in his elegant book, *Last Child in the Woods*, says, "Quite simply, when we deny our children nature, we deny them beauty" (p. 186). Babies deserve to connect with beauty as much as anyone. One of my favorite recurring moments of beauty when I am outside at Pacific Oaks is when the wind gusts and brings down a rain of small yellow leaves from the big Chinese elm tree. It is pure magic as the toddlers stop what they are doing and look up in a moment of wonder, crying "It's leafs!" or other exclamations of astonishment.

The toddlers, and younger ones as well, enjoy the sand, water, and rocks that are enhanced by a well-designed climbing structure in the Pacific Oaks Infant-Toddler yard. To this basic environment, my colleagues and I add balls, riding toys, shopping carts, buckets and shovels, small and large trucks, lots of vessels to hold and transfer sand and water, from ice cube trays to plastic or stainless steel bowls of all sizes to gallon milk jugs, and a changing assortment of small toy animals, which are usually classified by the logic of geography: jungle animals, farm animals, or ocean dwellers. However, occasionally the adults get bored and decide to classify differently, and the children find zebras, pandas, and penguins tucked in the sand and among the rocks (all black and white), or different species of "bears" (panda, polar, and brown). (Adults have to play, too, sometimes!) There is a Plexiglas easel, and paint is offered once the infants' compulsive orality

wanes somewhat. They will eat the paint, no matter what, and they will paint themselves as readily as the easel. This is everyone's favorite "photo op," in fact. (My associates and I use nontoxic washable tempera, and I do not mind plugging Lakeshore's brand as more washable than others.)

Except for a few things like soft-bodied dolls and puzzle pieces that could get lost in the sand, the toddlers are allowed to carry toys from inside to outside. Everything except paint, sand, and water from outside is allowed inside. This all means that there is a bit more cleanup, but it is worth it. My teammates and I do not want to be too restrictive about how the children use what is offered to them in the environment.

Quiet Observation

The last and really most important part of the environment that helps children to maximize their play is the appreciative attention of the adults who are responsible for the children. One of the unique features of a RIE parent–infant class (and other programs inspired by RIE) is the "quiet observation time" that is structured into the schedule. During this time, which is at least 20 minutes long and starts after adults and children have had a chance to "warm in," the adults stop talking among themselves, sit in a comfortable spot on the periphery, and give the children their undivided attention. Conversations started between parents and teachers during warming-in are put on hold. During this time, the adults respond to the children in a low-key way, if called on, but they do not initiate conversations or play. They simply watch and enjoy as the infants and/or toddlers explore the environment. This practice—which is called "wants nothing time" (Gerber, 1979, p. 21)—seems unnatural at first, as most of the adults are not generally accustomed to being together without talking except at a play or concert. However, to the children, it is a welcome relief not to have to spend any of their attention either screening out the general noise level of a bunch of adults talking and laughing or trying to understand what is being said. The children, my RIE colleagues and I perceive, are genuinely nourished by the freely offered gift of appreciative, noncoercive time and attention from their significant adults. Sometimes, the children choose to stay on the parent's lap, or very near the parent, for a while, just basking in the peaceful togetherness. However, eventually almost all will venture forth, trusting solidly that their "secure base" (Bowlby, 1988) is not going anywhere. During quiet time, children play with more concentration and engage in less conflict. (See box RIE Observation Time for more information on benefits of quiet observation.)

While orienting new groups of parents to this discipline, the analogy of therapy often comes up. Adults pay psychotherapists a lot of money to listen without judgment to help them feel better. With that in mind, Magda always said that if adults offer their nonjudgmental quiet attention to the children now, maybe they will not need therapy later on. After the observation period, there is a discussion about what happened during the 20 minutes. This discussion helps reinforce what the parents experienced watching the group because they learn so much about the competence and initiative of the children this way. If observation time does not happen for some reason on a given day, parents and teachers never feel quite as well connected to the children and each other. Talking is supposed to bring people together, and often it does, but shared silence of this nature adds a complementary bonding effect that enhances all of the relationships in the group.

It is possible to add the element of quiet observation to home as well as child care settings. At home, it is delicious to a baby or young child to have the parents' undivided, open-ended attention, during which it is the child's agenda, not the adult's, that is followed for 20 or 30 minutes. Observing my 8-month-old son in this way taught me more about the attention span of babies than all of the child development classes in the world. If I had not seen him playing with that tea strainer, uninterrupted for 11 minutes, I would not have believed it possible. Infant and toddler teachers can create the same kind of quiet opportunities for learning just by remembering not to chat throughout the day about things like what movie they saw last night while they are with the children. Of course they must talk about things concerning the program, but social chitchat over the heads of the babies lowers the quality of the care and attention the babies receive. This is really difficult to stick to all of the time, but it should be a program

RIE Observation Time

One of the most characteristic elements of RIE parent–infant classes, the centerpiece, is the structured quiet observation time. This is when, after a time to greet each other and "warm in," the facilitator asks the adults to stop talking among themselves and offer their full attention to the babies as they play for a period of 20 minutes or so. It is remarkable how difficult this is for many people; being quiet together is not something they are inclined, culturally, to do, especially with people they do not know well. However, with encouragement from the facilitator, who is there to keep the children safe while the parents sit back, this becomes, according to reports, their very favorite time of the week. In the midst of a hectic life, peacefully watching their own and others' children freely and joyfully exploring, with no agenda and no responsibility to make intelligent or witty conversation, especially among competitive types, is such a relief. They learn to trust their children, and themselves. Parents get positively hooked on this special time. Something magical happens when they all just sit and watch appreciatively; a new level of concentration emerges. During this protected interval the children make plans and execute them, they play with more skill at problem solving, they sometimes profoundly engage with one another, and have relatively few conflicts over toys. Often, they begin to vocalize, and the adults hear them echoing each other. If they "speak" to their parents, of course parents respond, but still refrain from talking to each other. The facilitator speaks to the children if intervention is needed, but not otherwise. This is a challenge for me as much as anyone, as I tend to chattiness, but when I discipline myself to observe quietly, the parents find that ability in themselves, too. They appreciate it, and miss it if it does not happen. Getting to know the children in this deep way, enfolding them in the circle of attention, almost feels sacred. It builds a group consciousness that all our talking time does not. Afterward, the adults are asked to talk about what they saw, and it does not have to be some important milestone to be excited over. Whatever happens, though, the uninterrupted regard they have paid sinks in so that the children know they have been seen and accepted. They have learned something about how to pay attention, by having attention paid to them (Hammond, 2004).

aspiration. A period of time to take notes on the children's actions and reactions each day is a good way to structure this quiet togetherness, and parents so appreciate the window into their little ones' days.

A Word About Health

More and more research shows that exposure in infancy to the microbes with which people normally share the world prepares the immune system to do its job well. (Brody, 2009; Ruebush, 2009) An aesthetically arranged classroom or play yard should be organized and tidy, and dirt should be in its place, when the children arrive. Certainly, basic hygienic practices like hand washing at appropriate times must be followed. However, and this, again, involves an unmistakable cultural per-spective, children who are allowed to play outdoors freely in a rich environment are usually quite a messy sight by the end of the day. It is not stretching the truth to say that the dirtier, wetter, and messier they end up, the more fun they have had and the more they have learned that will serve them later in life. If parents of children in child care are unable to appreciate this, because they either do not understand or agree or do not have the resources to handle so much laundry, perhaps the program can maintain a cupboard of play clothes that can be changed into at the beginning of the day and out of at the end. Vessels that get drunk out of during play are put in the dishwasher at the end of the day, as are the shovels and used chew toys. Anything known to have been "slimed" gets washed, and everything else gets wiped down as needed.

Naturally, the usual illnesses get passed around, like colds and other viruses, but as long as I have been at RIE and Pacific Oaks, there has never been an outbreak of anything serious, thanks to modern vaccines, nor of one that could have been avoided by changing standard practices. I empathize with every program director who has had to contend with frus-trated parents whose child has come down with her fourth cold in 7 weeks and must explain that keeping her inside really does not eliminate illness, and that you cannot keep her away from water play and the other children all day. The best that can be done (knowing I have "been there" with my own child at some point) is to listen with love, understanding that there is absolutely no way to keep young children from exposing one another to the common germs, especially as contagion often arises before symptoms. It is an unavoidable hazard of gathering children in groups, but the benefits, social and immunological, are worth it in the long run.

Outcomes of Free Play

If a baby receives the proper balance, for his temperament, of sensitive caregiving, loving, playful attention during noncare interactions, and the opportunity to move freely and explore creatively in a rich environment, he will be ready to tackle adult-initiated academic tasks when the time comes. When that time should come is one of the never-ending discussions between people who know the value of play and those who are not convinced of it. Of course, RIE casts its vote with the play-as-preparation-for-academics side, but that does not mean children are sheltered from academic experiences that are compelling to them. My colleagues and I would not make an infant or toddler sit to be read to if he is not interested, but would like the child to have experiences with books when he is ready for some lap time. RIE practitioners are not inclined to "test" children endlessly with questions while they are playing ("Where's the yellow one? Can you put the yellow one in? Where does the yellow one go? What shape is it?"), but the question-and-answer format is a nice way to look at a book with a preliterate, preverbal child who can point and do sound effects ("Where's the mama dog? What's the puppy say?"). I think the difference in conversational interplay between a RIE-influenced adult–child dyad has to do with the faith the adult has in the child's intrinsic motivation to learn (Pinto, 1995). If the adult trusts the child to want to know things, and believes in his ability to synthesize meaning, then those questions that seem like "testing" are more playful, less pressured, and more child responsive. If, on the other hand, we think we must "teach" in order for children to learn, they will be more worried about getting right answers than in learning. Is it possible for adults to know precisely what children need to know next as they are constructing their inner representation and understanding of their experiences? If adults are excellent observers, they might be able to provide just the exact lesson the child would benefit from once in awhile. However, if adults really trust children's instincts for learning, the children will find out what they need to know next by following their interests (Jones & Reynolds, 1992).

For me and for many RIE parents and practitioners, this is a great comfort, because the pressure is lifted. What adults need to do most is care for children sensitively, observe their explorations with interest and appreciation, and enjoy their discoveries with them, without intrusively overwhelming them with praise, judgments, or other agendas. This approach leads to the establishment of self-confidence that is so often recognized in babies, toddlers, and children who have had RIE in their lives from the beginning.

References

Bowlby, J. (1988). *A secure base*. New York: Basic Books.

Brody, J. (2009, January 27). Babies know: A little dirt is good for you. *The New York Times*. Retrieved February 4, 2009, from http://query.nytimes.com/gst/fullpage.html?res = 9C01EFD71231F934A15752C0A96F9C8B63&sec = &spon = &pagewanted = 1

Erikson, E. H. (1950). *Childhood and society.* New York: W.W. Norton & Co.

Erikson, J. (1988). *Wisdom and the senses.* New York: W.W. Norton & Co.

Gerber, M. (Ed.). (1979). *The RIE manual for parents and professionals.* Los Angeles: Resources for Infant Educarers.

Gerber, M. (2002). *Dear parent: Caring for infants with respect, expanded edition.* Los Angeles: Resources for Infant Educarers.

Hammond, R.A. (2004). Paying attention. *Educaring, 24*(1 & 2), 1–8.

Hammond, R. A. (2007). Playing with babies: The baby is not the toy. *Educaring 28*(1), 1–6.

Jones, E., & Cooper, R.(2005). *Playing to get smart.* New York: Teachers College Press.

Jones, E., & Reynolds, G. (1992). *The play's the thing: Adult's roles in children's play.* New York: Teacher's College Press.

Kálló, E., & Balog, G. (2005). *The origins of free play.* Budapest, Hungary: The Pikler Institute.

Kovach, B., & Da Ros-Voseles, D. (2008). *Being with babies: Understanding and responding to the infants in your care.* Beltsville, MD: Gryphon House.

Louv, R. (2005). *Last child in the woods: Saving our children from nature-deficit disorder.* New York: Algonquin Books of Chapel Hill.

New Oxford Dictionary of English. (1998). New York: Oxford University Press.

Piaget, J. (1964). Development and learning. In Frank B. Murray (Ed.), *Critical features of Piaget's theory of the development of thought* (1972; 57–67). New York: MSS Information Corporation.

Pikler, E. (1969). Peaceful babies—Contented mothers. In M. A. Roche (Ed.), *Sensory Awareness Foundation Bulletin, 14*, 5–24 1994.

Pinto, C. (1995). Is faster better? *Educaring, 16,*(1&2), p. 4–5.

Rogoff, B. (2003). *The cultural nature of human development.* New York: Oxford University Press.

Ruebush, M. (2009). *Why dirt is good: 5 ways to make dirt your friend.* New York: Kaplan.

White, B. L. (1975). *The first three years of life.* Englewood Clifffs, NJ: Prentice Hall, Inc.

Zigler, E. F., Singer, D. G., & Bishop-Josef, S. J. (Eds.). (2004). *Children's play: The roots of reading.* Washington, DC: ZERO TO THREE.

Chapter 8

Babies and Toddlers Together

One of the most challenging things about working with infants and toddlers, and the most interesting, is facilitating interactions between them. Everyone would love it if the children could "all just get along," but it is an unrefutable fact that human beings are often in conflict with one another, and babies and toddlers are no exception. Sometimes adults even hold babies to a higher standard than they hold themselves, expecting empathy and altruism from tiny people who do not even have their sense of self constructed yet. Because RIE practitioners try not to undercut their ego formation by aggressively overriding very young children's healthy impulses to explore and experiment, the RIE approach sometimes seems counterintuitive. It may look like RIE is promoting a self-indulgent free-for-all, with no rules of proper behavior in evidence, because the children are allowed to take toys from each other and engage in noisy tugs-of-war. However, over time, RIE practices facilitate their knowledge about their own likes and dislikes, their sense of personal power, how their actions affect others, and, ultimately, that cooperation and negotiation are more effective in extending play and friendship than selfishness.

There are no hard and fast rules of what Magda Gerber called "selective intervention" (Gerber, 2002), but rather guiding principles to consider when choosing to intervene. In any given situation, there might be a hierarchy of values that must instantly be prioritized. Therefore, a facilitator must use her intuition to assess the best way to apply the guidelines on the spot—based on the specifics of the present events and environment, past experience, and knowledge of the children—then hope (and pray!) that the intervention will bring the children a little closer to a mature self-appreciation as well as respect for others, even if it does not bring an immediate resolution. It is important to note that no two RIE-inspired facilitators would do or say exactly the same things in the same situation; each has her personal style and pre-ferred values. However, there will be some similarities, based on the guiding principles. The first guiding principle is that infants and toddlers need support and information, not judgment. See if you can glean from the following pages what some of the other principles are.

First Contact

It is surprising to see how much really tiny babies enjoy the opportuni-ty to be near one another. Babies who sometimes have a difficult time playing on the floor or in a playpen on their own are often content to lie on their backs and learn to play when there are little friends nearby to observe. Whether it is in an informal playgroup, a RIE Parent–Infant

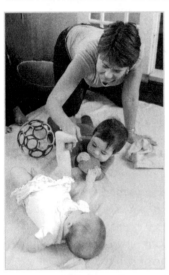

Guidance class, or a child care program, by the time babies are 3 months old, they can be placed on a sheet-covered rug or mat with a few strategically placed simple toys and a few similarly skilled compan-ions. If trusted adults are nearby to offer a sense of security, they can play happily for amazingly long periods of time, and eventually, while working on their move-ment skills, they will discover one another. It is breathtaking to be present for this first contact.

Usually, it is the first baby in a group to turn over onto its tummy who initiates the first interaction, often accidentally rolling next to or onto a neighbor. A very sensitive neighbor might be startled and protest, but as often as not, the response is more welcoming (Vincze & Appell, 2000). Adults are often too quick to separate the babies. A RIE facilitator would, if there seemed to be a problem, move in slowly, communicating calm appreciation of the situa-tion in her body language and tone of voice. She might say, "Lucia, I see Alejandro has come very close to you; you seem upset. I will help him give you some space." Then she would say, "Alejandro, Lucia is crying because you are so close. I would like to move you a little further from her." Then she would wait for Alejandro to prepare his body to be moved, which could be seen with careful observation, and slowly lift and move him. If Lucia is still upset at this point, then the adult would try to help her "reset" to a calm, ready-to-play attitude by offering a few words, a pat, or, if necessary, a few moments of cuddling.

Of course, if Lucia had not reacted negatively, the facilitator would not need to intervene, although it might be helpful for her to narrate the action a little, to give both infants a sense of security and a little information to support their learning. This could be a statement as simple and brief as, "Oh, Alejandro, you found Lucia!" At some point it might be necessary to move them apart again, but not until they have had a chance to be together.

Is It a Person or a Thing?

After babies start to really notice one another, the first physical contact gives way to something more—genuine connection can be seen between two babies who gaze into one another's eyes with wonder. It is difficult not to suspect that they know it is someone not something. However, they are likely to experiment with the other baby as though he were an object. That is when the adult very quietly and selectively facilitates a gentle approach. If Shahrzad wants to touch those sparkly blue objects she is gazing into (Adam's eyes), I will move in and say, "Those are Adam's eyes. If you poke, it hurts him." I will couple my words with action; I will touch Shahrzad's face, near her eyes, as I gently guide her hand to a less vulnerable part of Adam's face. I will add the word "gentle" or "softly" to my actions. If Shahrzad still needs to touch eyes, I will bring her a doll and tell her she can touch the doll's eyes. In like fashion, if the issue is hair pulling, a doll with "real" hair is a handy tool (as seen demonstrated by Magda in *With Care and Respect: On Their Own With Our Help*; Gerber & Forrest, 1978).

Just being near, not rushing in to separate the infants, and offering safe ways to touch lets the infants know that we value their interest in one another, and that we trust them to be together. As always, safety is the first priority, but not startling them by overreacting is a close second. If facilitators are uptight about the babies' first interactions, they pick up on that, which adds tension to their initiations, and this is exactly what we try to avoid. RIE practitioners want to project, right from the beginning, that being with others is a peaceful and pleasurable state.

As babies get a little older, into toddlerhood, and start to act in ways that seem to be motivated by aggressive or angry impulses, using the same approach is not appropriate, because it does not address their authentic feelings. If Eloise is feeling angry that her mother just told her no about something, and strikes out at the nearest playmate, saying, "Gentle, gentle" will not add to Eloise's emotional intelligence. When potentially hurtful acts are not done as part of innocent exploration, then the facilitator needs to address what seems to be happening. Therefore, I would say, "Eloise, it seems you are angry, but I can't let you hit Geoffrey. Is there another way you can show your feelings that won't hurt anyone?" I would stay close until I knew for sure that she had calmed down. The presence of an adult who accepts all of their feelings can, of itself, offer scaffolding for the self-calming that young children need to learn.

Helpful Conditions

The important thing in facilitating interactions between infants is to intervene selectively. The old saying, "If it ain't broke, don't fix it," comes to mind. There are several factors that make it easier to be relaxed about letting interactions happen naturally.

First, it helps if the infants who are together on the mat are close both in size and ability to move around. This is why, when consulting with child care providers, RIE recommends grouping infants and toddlers of similar gross motor stages. Of course, infants all develop at their own pace, so it is impossible to have a group that stays perfectly matched over time. If you are going to be able to focus your attention on the child you are diapering or feeding, then you have to be able to trust that the other infants or toddlers playing together in their play area are not terribly mismatched in size and strength.

This poses a challenge for home child care providers, who often have mixed-age groups, but it can be overcome by the second factor that helps promote peaceful interactions—an environment that is carefully planned. Toddlers and young infants should not be left in the same space without careful supervision. Whether by accident or design, it is a fact that toddlers can hurt infants. In any mixed-age setting, it makes all the difference to provide young infants with a gated off play area so that the older children cannot be freely moving in and through their space (Kálló & Balog, 2005). Although playpens are too restrictive for infants who are really moving around, they are a perfectly fine place for infants who are not yet rolling, especially if they can provide a safety zone when older children present a hazard.

This separation of toddlers from infants promotes peacefulness by letting the environment set the limits, rather than the adult, making the adult's job much easier and taking the danger out of the situation. This is safer—physically and psychologically—for older and younger children alike. Jealous impulses, which many toddlers have about infants, or simple curiosity-induced mistakes are to be expected. ("Hmmm . . . what will happen if I throw this book at the baby?")

Safety was always Magda's first priority. Many times I have heard her answer, when parents would say, "Oh, that's never happened," about a potential safety hazard. "Not yet" was Magda's comeback.

So, the first consideration for promoting positive interactions between babies is grouping them similarly in a safe, well-planned space with an adult nearby who facilitates calmly and selectively. Having an attitude of trust in the infants' ability to handle their feelings when conflicts come up, and not imposing adult notions of justice, are essential to maintaining this calm approach. Babies are usually more interested than upset when another baby takes a toy away from them. There is a lot of passing back and forth of toys in which no intervention is needed. RIE facilitators observe this behavior without comment until such time that there is unhappiness associated with it. If a child seems sad or upset, another similar toy can be calmly offered or pointed out, and this may be sufficient. If the baby is still unhappy, a simple reflection of his displeasure and a little information are enough: "Oh, you liked that bangle, and Jack took it. He likes it, too. Now you seem sad." It is about the feelings, not the object.

A tug-of-war over a toy can really get emotions going, both in the children and in the adults. It is helpful for adults to connect with their own feelings about fairness and right and wrong. Some cultures and some families hold a higher value of private ownership; some value collective ownership more. It is my belief that either attitude toward ownership is somewhat irrelevant to toddlers. To children not yet acculturated to economic systems, the relevant concept is usership, not ownership. It is more important for them to learn to identify what interests them than who "owns" what. The larger cultural values will come through implicitly in what children see the adults around them doing and explicitly when they are old enough for complex conversations. The value of sharing cannot be overemphasized, and I think an attitude of generosity in a family has far-reaching effects on children. However, generosity and truly altruistic actions develop over time and with maturity out of authentic caring for others.

Forcing very young children to act in ways that they do not feel does not serve the value of authenticity. Making children share before they can understand it is, in a sense, abusing adults' power over them to make ourselves feel better. Allowing a child to learn about how it feels to have a toy taken, how it feels to inspire another child to cry by taking her toy, how it feels to see the other child calm down when she voluntarily gives it back, these are the lessons that build understanding. It is personal; it is messy; it brings up a lot of emotion in adults. Letting children learn by doing pays off as they construct real knowledge about the social world and their place in it.

Justice Comes Later

In group situations, it is helpful for adults to let go of the notions of ownership and who had it first. They often miss the first stages of a conflict, and when they are working with preverbal or newly verbal children, the emotions are much more important to mediate than the facts. With younger infants, it is easy to manage a conflict over a toy by making sure that there are enough toys to go around, with multiples of the most popular ones. (Of course, sometimes this is an unaffordable luxury.) Very young infants usually do not react negatively at all when another baby takes their toys away. The interaction is often of more interest to them than the toy, and they will quickly find a different object that makes them just as happy.

When they get a little older, and a little more passionate about their play, it minimizes conflict and increases group accord if adults can offer a substitute and say, "I see you both want this ball. I'll go find some more balls." If there are not more balls, or if another ball will not do, then adults have to talk about the feelings: "Oh, Jamie, you are upset; Melissa took the ball. Melissa, Jamie is crying because you took the ball. He didn't like that." Two messages are being relayed. First, I am letting Jamie know I understand him. Second, I'm modeling empathy for Melissa and giving her information about the consequences of her action. What I am not doing is trying to fix it.

If I take the ball away from Melissa to give it back to Jamie, then I am modeling that it is okay to take toys because I am doing it. In addition, I am not acknowledging Melissa's equal passion for the ball. By not rushing to rescue Jamie, I am also giving him the opportunity to find his own way to make himself happy again. This is how I encourage his ability to self-regulate. I do not pick him up and waltz him around the room to distract him or wave a lot of other toys in his face. If I say, "I'm sorry you're sad. I wonder what else you can find to play with," I am letting him know that I have faith in his ability to solve his problem.

Special Considerations

If a child in a group has a special need that requires more adult intervention to level the playing field or to manage emotions, this will give the group a bit different balance of adult-driven versus child-driven problem solving. It is always imperative to individualize an intervention to the particular situation and children involved; it is not about rules yet. You do not work off of a script, if you want to meet each child's needs. In fact, any child's level of need is a fluid thing. One day a child can handle his emotions easily, whereas on another day, after a wakeful night, he needs more adult help to gain emotional balance. The adult adjusts her interventions to fit the child, wherever the child is on the continuum of need. With sensitivity, facilitators can guide toddlers to genuine consideration for their classmates however able they are to move around or to grasp social complexities. Respect is for everybody.

For instance, if Trace, who is autistic, pushes Kathryn at the snack table, I will handle it the same way I would if Trace were not autistic: "Trace, Kathryn is eating her snack. She doesn't like to be pushed." Then I would remind Kathryn that Trace needs extra space around him, and tell her I need to move her stool a little. When a child is less mobile than the others, I will make sure the others do not take off with all of the toys within reach, saying, "I don't want you to take Jessie's ball. She needs toys to play with, and she can't go get them yet. Would you like to stay here and play with her, or find another ball?" (This is a tactic that works well with older and younger siblings, too.)

Whose Problem Is It, Anyway?

Here is my guiding principle: As the adult, I want to make sure I am there to solve all of the adult-size problems for children: making sure there are enough toys to go around, that food arrives before they get too hungry, or that naptime comes when it should. Beyond that, to encourage infants and toddlers to use their inner resourcefulness, I may consult on their baby-sized problems, "What can I play with now?" or "How can I push this cart over the curb?" but I will not try to solve them. I believe they can do it. I trust them to succeed.

This is another way the RIE philosophy really helps adults relax and enjoy being with infants and toddlers more. It is very stressful to think it is our job to make sure they are always smiling and happy. If adults accept that life brings challenges, and challenges bring not only tears but also important learning opportunities, they can be on the child's wavelength without over-empathizing. They will not be tying themselves into knots to make sure everyone is happy all of the time. No one is happy all of the time. That is life, even for babies and toddlers. The irony is that if adults try too hard to make them happy, it actually interferes with their ability to be happy. Have you ever known a person who seems to think it is your job to make sure he is fulfilled and content at all times, or blames others for his problems? If you have, I bet that you resented that sense of misplaced responsibility. Balance is the key. All people need others who care about them and want them to be happy, but it is easier to be together when each person takes responsibility for his own happiness. How adults facilitate the growth of children's emotional intelligence can make a huge difference in their attitudes and expectations in the midst of life's ups and downs.

Toddler Tussles

A RIE playgroup with seven toddlers between the ages of 2 and 3 years is in session. The parents are chatting under the shade in the outside play yard while I, as facilitator, clean up after snack and the toddlers are getting busy again. Gina, the oldest child in the group, at 2¾ years, has gone over to where the purses, diaper bags, and paraphernalia have been put down on a bench. She finds Elena's lovely pair of shiny turquoise sneakers sitting there, looking most attractive. Gina climbs up and sits on the bench, and spends a long time working diligently to put the shoes on. She is very happy with the results of her effort, and comes back across the yard to show her mother, Annette. However, 2-year-old Elena sees what Gina is wearing on her feet and is outraged. Elena bursts into tears, yelling, "Take them off! My shoes! Mine! Mine!"

As facilitator, I move in and say, "Gina, Elena is crying because you are wearing her shoes, and she doesn't want you to." I then say to Elena, "Elena, Gina will give you back your shoes when she is finished wearing them. She likes your shoes. They are pretty. I won't let her do anything to harm them." Elena continues wailing, unappeased, and Gina looks at her with interest. She looks at her mommy, who is looking at Elena with a worried expression. Gina says something, which only another one of the mothers is able to hear over Elena's cries, and she sits down and assists Gina in taking off the shoes. Gina's mother is not seeing this because she is saying to me, "Why didn't you make her give them back right away?" I am formulating my answer as the tide turns.

Gina gives the shoes to Elena, rather graciously, I think. If Gina is sad to give up the shoes, she does not show it so much. However, she is paying close attention to all of the adults standing around her. She receives a round of thanks from the mothers, and I say, "You gave them back to Elena. That made her happy. Thank you."

In answer to Annette's question—why I did not insist on Gina giving back the shoes immediately—I open my mouth to speak, but Elena's dad, Carlos, and the other parents start the job for me. They explain to her that if I had forced Gina, she would have been deprived of the opportunity to return the shoes voluntarily. She would have been given the idea that the adults found her untrustworthy. In addition, she would have incorporated a sense that "might makes right," that the bigger and more powerful person in any interaction is the one who gets her or his way. I chime in that Elena was also educated by this experience, in that she learned the world is not always just as she would like it, and that adults are not always going to fix it. However, she might have learned that adults are going to care about her feelings and the feelings of the other child as well. She discovered that Gina is an essentially reasonable person, who heard what Elena had to say and acted on it. It was a rich learning experience for both toddlers, and the adults as well.

However, even if Gina had not taken off the shoes right away, there would have been positive lessons in the exchange, in the long run. At some point, people all have to learn that even if they do not get things their way sometimes, there are other options open to them. If that had happened, I would have said to Elena, "I wonder what you could do to have fun until Gina is ready to take your shoes off." I would not overwhelm her with suggestions, though. Usually, suggestions only build defensiveness. Toddlers are more likely to exercise an option they have thought of themselves.

Sometimes It Is Not About the Toy

Toddlers are challenging to raise and care for because they are so ready to test their power in the world but are just beginning to develop judgement. Power is a very important issue for them, whether it is within themselves ("How strong am I? Can I move this couch?"), with adults ("Do I really have to do what you say, or will you negotiate?"), or with their peers ("Who is stronger? Can I hold my own?"). This need to test themselves in the context of relationships with other children is a very important task, and one that requires sensitive support from adults in order to build mutual respect between children. A perfect example of a toddler power struggle arose the very next week between Gina and Elena, which then carried over to the next week in terms of real learning.

At the Plexiglas easel, where there are three paint cups and three brushes, Gina is painting with warm beige tempera. Elena arrives and wastes no time in grabbing hold of the brush in Gina's hand. Gina holds on tight and says, "No, that's my brush." In spite of the slippery paint, their tug-of-war continues. I come near and point to the other brushes, saying, "Gina is using that brush, Elena. There are other brushes right here. There are enough for both of you." Elena says, "No, this brush." She pulls harder and manages to wrench it away from Gina. Elena runs across the yard, with Gina in pursuit. I follow. My goal here is not to stop the conflict, but just to see that it does not result in anyone getting hurt. Both girls have a grip on the brush, and another unheeded reminder that there are more lets me know that this is not about the brush, but about the relationship. So I go into "sportscasting" mode (see Averting Conflict Through Sportscasting section) and say, "You are both pulling hard. You both want the same brush. I am here to keep you safe. I don't want anyone to get hurt." My fear is that if one lets go, the other will catapult backward and fall over. I have a hand on the backs of both girls as I calmly narrate. They are both pulling so hard their muscles are shaking and their faces are grim. I am impressed with their physical strength, and their strength of will. After quite a while, Gina gets the brush and goes near her mother, but Elena follows and the tugging starts again. Elena is crying very loudly; she is really, really angry. One big tug gives Gina the advantage, and Elena runs up the ramp of the climbing structure, absolutely distraught until she sees the four small toy dogs that she loves to find in the yard and calls out, "My puppies, Papí, my puppies!" A radiant smile shines through her tears; the paintbrush no longer exists. Gina is relieved, but does not return to painting. She moves on to other interests. I am relieved, too, because the girls are so well matched that the struggle might have gone on all day and because I am glad for the parents to see that neither girl is destroyed by the conflict. Within a few minutes they are playing peacefully side by side at the water table.

The following week Carlos, Elena's father, tells me that in the car on the way to class Elena mentioned the paintbrush. He reflected back to her, "You and Gina were both pulling on the paintbrush. But how many paintbrushes were there?" Elena replied, "Two." Carlos said, "Actually, *Gorda*, there were three paintbrushes." Then after a beat, Elena said to her father, "Today, I am going to use the other brush."

Elena's decision is just what I had anticipated would come of the incident—a gut-level realization that it is not worth fighting over the brush. There were no conflicts between Gina and Elena that day, and neither one of them had been told to just "be nice."

Averting Conflict Through Sportscasting

Five toddlers are having a grand time playing in an empty plastic swimming pool with a built-in slide. The pool is about 4 feet in diameter, and I have put some balls of various sizes in the pool to add interest. The enthusiasm is rising; the game has evolved and defined itself. They are sliding down, wiggling at the bottom then climbing out and running back for a repeat. Twenty little arms and legs are being flung in every direction and squeals of excitement are bursting out of five happy mouths. It is looking dangerous now, like somebody is bound to get seriously bumped.

One script in my head is urging me to rush over to the group and say, "Hey, kids, settle down, now! Someone's going to get hurt!" However, I love that they are so excited and really mixing it up with each other. The parents and I have been looking forward to this kind of groupness since September (it is now May), and I do not want to squelch their glee. However, I do want them to be safe. Fortunately, I have a technique that usually works in this type of situation without repressing the play. In fact, it extends and enriches the play. So I move over by the pool and go into sportscasting mode.

I begin to describe the action. "Oh, Claire is climbing up behind Anton...Anton is standing at the top. Careful, Claire, he might fall if you push...Cameron and Dominic are being silly together; they're pretending to swim at the bottom...Here comes Anton! Whee! Watch your feet!...Dustin is tugging on the side of the pool. It's heavy, isn't it, with everyone inside it?"

So many program goals have been met in this rowdy scenario, and I have not once said, "No," "You have to take turns," or "You can't climb up the slide, you have to go around" or told them, "You're are going to get hurt." (In general, children will do what adults say, so if we tell them they are going to get hurt, they probably will.)

There are so many levels of richness going on in this collaboration. The toddlers are learning that they can have fun together and coordinate their actions and intentions. They have entered a whole new level of motor planning. My words are scaffolding their attention to one another so that their body-awareness expands to include their friends. In addition, they see that I approve and support this play. I am laughing with them, and they can see that I am all for joyful arousal! However, they sense that I am there to keep them safe, which provides a wonderful juxtaposition of pleasure and security in togetherness. To add some icing on this delicious cake, the toddlers are also getting a language and sequencing lesson through my sportscast. I have intervened, but I have not intruded. I have been included, and I have thoroughly enjoyed my morning.

Sportscasting is especially useful when there are toddlers who have a difficult time sharing space with other children and are prone to push or bite. It is good in any situation where there is a lot of toddler traffic, like at the sensory table. This technique is a great way of guiding interactions that is totally nonjudgmental and helps adults hone their observation skills. The adults are not presuming that they know the best course of action, but are leaving the door open to the children's creative solutions. The best part is, it is easy; you just say what you see, and usually the toddlers will do the rest.

When You Must Just Say No

Of course, there are times when an adult has got to intervene more directly. The more descriptive approach like that taken with Elena and Gina does not always work, especially when a child has figured out that she can take any toy she wants by yanking hard enough or moving in quickly enough. In cases like these, it seems that children have found their power and are asking, through their serial grabbing "Is that really OK? Can I really do this?" Then, the child needs to hear that, in fact, it is not acceptable to take toys from other children without their consent. Not all children pass through this stage, which comes up sometime after 18 or 20 months of age, but toddlers who do will move out of it fairly quickly if an adult facilitates closely (some call it "shadowing") for a while, until they learn that this sort of interaction will not be allowed to succeed. It is important to take a proactive approach so that the child will not get labeled as aggressive or a bully, with one thing compounding another. Preserving a child's self-esteem while reshaping her behavior is a challenging yet deeply rewarding enterprise for a facilitator.

To nip any growing negative reputation in the bud, it is helpful to assign one person, who is willing to forego negative judgments about the child, to become a compassionate companion until the difficulty is overcome. In facilitating this situation, it is necessary to anticipate when the child is about to go for another child's toy, and say something like, "I wonder what is here for you to play with that is not already in use," or simply, "He's using that now." If I get there too late, then I will ask him to return the toy to the other child and find something else to play with. Of course, toddlers have pride, too, and if he refuses to return the toy, I will then follow up with a bit of an ultimatum: "You can give the toy back to Jordan, because he was using it, or I will help you give it back. I won't let you play with it." I hope that the child's sense of autonomy will dictate that he give it back on his own, but if not, then I will gently but firmly take the toy away to give it back to the other child. My body and my voice must not communicate anger or violence, however, or I will just be reinforcing aggression. I do not judge the child; I merely guide his actions.

This does bring up some contradictory issues, but who ever said teaching toddlers was uncomplicated? On the one hand, I want the child whose toy was taken to be empowered to hold on tight and not lose the toy in the first place, but that did not happen. I also want that child to be able to express his feelings to the toy-taking child. I will facilitate that as best I can. However, on the hierarchy of values when facilitating toddler interactions, the priority must go to helping the child who is habitually taking toys to move past that. Just letting it go will not facilitate movement through this stage. The impulse to grab must be transformed, and one essential ingredient is to remove the rewards for the toy taking.

Being allowed to use the toy is somewhat but not completely gratifying. Seeing the emotional hubbub the behavior creates is exciting and often the most rewarding consequence, negative attention being better than no attention. Therefore, shadowing the child gives him attention during neutral behavior or prosocial interactions, lessening the need to create conflict to gain adult attention. It also eliminates the "charge" of getting another child upset, and of the use of ill-gotten gains.

If toy taking was the only problem, that would be great. However, in many child care and preschool programs, whether children are surrounded by violence in their neighborhoods or homes, or not, toddler aggression can take some serious and upsetting forms. Hitting, biting, kicking, and pushing are real. When teachers are challenged to keep all children safe in a program that includes children with recurring tendencies to hurt others, it is easy to start thinking of them as little criminals. However, there are no criminal behaviors among toddlers, and there should be no criminal reputations, either.

Toddlers behave aggressively for all the same reasons adults do, including fear, fatigue, hunger, needs not being met, feeling disrespected or frustrated, feeling encroached upon, jealousy, or having out-of-balance brain chemistry. Looking for causes and working to eliminate them is my primary approach to toddler aggression, whether it is a momentary stage or habitual. It is a "least harmful" assumption to presume that a toddler would behave better if, at that moment, she could. Rather than shaming, judging, or punishing, the best approach is to figure out how to make the environment feel safe to the child. Sometimes, the first response needs to be making sure the other children are safe from the aggressor. A statement that seems to make sense to toddlers is, "I don't want you to hurt [name of child], and I don't want anyone to hurt you. All of the children need to feel safe here. You, too." So, even if a child comes from a difficult home or neighborhood, adults can try to mitigate that by making the child care or school setting feel easy and safe.

This may sometimes mean temporarily and creatively isolating a child who feels overwhelmed by the social requirements of group living. Isolation may seem like punishment or shaming, depending on one's attitude. It does not have to feel that way to the child, if it is done with compassion. Giving a child some personal space may feel liberating. Or, some "time in" with a caring adult who will invite the child to help with a task, play with him, or pay attention while he plays independently can give him a chance to reset his nervous system.

When a conflict occurs, the faster-than-conscious right hemisphere of the brain alerts a person to potential threats in the environment. The sympathetic nervous system is activated and arousal is heightened. If a toddler in an aroused state is further excited by the adult's intervention (e.g., loudly insisting the child give the toy back), the toddler's fight-or-flight response will certainly kick in more intensely. However, if an adult moves in with calm "holding" of the whole situation, without inducing high levels of shame, and her words match the feelings of the child ("You really want to hold that truck tightly, don't you?"), the adult is scaffolding for the child, helping him to understand the nature of his excitation, and, with synchrony achieved, allowing his aggressive arousal to lessen. As the parasympathetic nervous system is activated through the kindness of the adult, he begins to calm down; his logical left brain has a chance to process that there is another truck across the room he could have. All of this applies to the other child in the interaction as well, the so-called victim. In well-mediated instances such as these, the child's bodily experience, which is the underpinning of his mind, gets practice in managing the fight, flight, or freeze response to threat. He will learn that a typical everyday threat can be managed. This confidence will become built into the psychobiology of his nervous system. It is when threats to the child are unmediated and pro-longed or chronic, compounded by high levels of shaming, as can occur in poor-quality child care, that the child may become overly sensitized to threat, habitually overreacting to harmless interactions with others, possi-bly resulting in long-term negative consequences on his ability to manage the normal stresses of human interaction (Schore, 1994).

Fortunately, a child can have a secure attachment with a teacher or caregiver, even if life at home is chaotic and anxiety producing, which gives adults all the more motivation to connect with a child who has diffi-culty with self-control. If everyone just gives up on a toddler who is acting out by expelling her from the program, this increases the risk that a child will be labeled for life. A well-trained child care teacher can make a world of difference.

In summing up the RIE approach to the facilitation of interactions between infants and toddlers, the watchword is "wait." By waiting we allow their ideas to emerge. If an intervention then seems necessary, it will be an informed action rather than a hasty reaction. This thoughtful manner is modeling the message RIE parents and professionals want to teach. Toddlers who have experienced this way of being together since infancy are surprisingly competent problem-solvers and display enthusi-asm and tenderness for their peers. More than once parents have told me that their toddlers regularly include their RIE class friends and teachers in their bedtime remembrances.

References

Gerber, M. (2002). *Dear parent: Caring for infants with respect* (expanded edition). Los Angeles: Resources for Infant Educarers.

Gerber, M., & Forrest, T. (1978). *With care and respect: On their own with our help* [Video/DVD]. Los Angeles: Resources for Infant Educarers.

Kálló, E., & Balog, G. (2005). *The origins of free play.* Budapest, Hungary: The Pikler Institute.

Schore, A. N. (1994). *Affect regulation and the origin of the self: The neurobiology of emotional development.* Hillsdale, NJ: Erlbaum.

Vincze, M., & Appell, G. (2000). *Babies and young children with each other* [DVD]. Budapest, Hungary: The Pikler Institute.

Chapter 9

Learning to Pay Attention: Entertainment Versus Engagement

*An essential function of adults is to manage the sensory environ-
ment so that the infant receives the optimal amount and kinds of
stimulation. When there is too much or the wrong type of input,
the infant is likely to tune out or become agitated. When there is
too little, she may become frustrated with boredom and either give
up her natural curiosity or become demanding and cranky. Either
mismatch causes the infant to miss out on learning opportunities.
If stimulation is regularly of the "entertainment" variety, the baby
may become a habitually passive recipient who expects always to
be entertained, rather than an active investigator. With appropriate sources and levels of sensory stimulation, which include
interactions with people, objects, movement, music, light, and
shadow, the infant will satisfy herself by engaging in a wide
range of exploratory behaviors that are self-initiated and allow her
to manage her attention as her increasing understanding and the
environment intersect.*

Infants are able to pay attention to the important elements in their lives
right from the beginning. I was present at the birth of my goddaughter,
and it was amazing to see her snap her little head to look toward her
father, who was speaking to her from across the room for the very first

time in the outside world. Her movement was clearly intentional; his voice obviously had meaning for her, a 1-minute-old baby. There have been many studies to examine the development of intentional—endogenous—attention in infants and young children because it is widely recognized that the voluntary control of awareness is an essential ingredient for cognition and learning (Colombo & Cheatham, 2006). The studies are often arranged to test how long infants will look at an object, with and without distraction, and there seems to be a point, around 9 months of age, when it is obvious that infants are deliberately screening out distractions to keep inspecting an object of interest. However, the studies do not measure attention to the internal world or factors that may lead to more sophisticated attentional self-organization (Williamson & Anzalone, 2001).

Although many products are sold to distract infants from their internal sensations (e.g., vibrating bouncy seats) or to stimulate looking behavior (e.g., crib mobiles), little attention is paid to how adults help or hinder infants from integrating their various senses into the useful ability to focus at will to follow a line of inquiry or to solve a problem. A wonderful, comprehensive system for actively fostering this type of attention in infants and toddlers can be found in the RIE and Pikler practices (Gerber, 1979, 2002; Roche, 1994).

The "first cause" in this effort is adults' observation of infants, through which they become more and more aware of how easy it is to interrupt a baby, and less and less inclined to do so unnecessarily. This does not mean that adults think infants can get along without them—certainly not. As practitioners are learning from neurobiology and regulation theorists such as Allan Schore (1994, 2003) and Jeree Pawl (2006), infants depend heavily on an adult partner to help them learn to regulate themselves over time. RIE practitioners have been operating from this paradigm for decades, and it is exciting to find that neuroscience is supporting the empirical evidence of this process that they have long observed. The quality of the caregiver's attention provides the model for the infant's ability to self-regulate, which includes the ability to productively pay attention.

The word *attention* derives from the word *attend*, which means, fundamentally, "to be present" (*Oxford Illustrated Dictionary*, 1998). Behaviorally, this means that the adult is fully attuned to and mindful of what the baby is experiencing as he is moved about, cared for, and stimulated. A mindful caregiver tries to make certain that levels of stimulation, whether from within or without, are not under- or overwhelming. Paying attention to the loved adult, of course, occurs during all kinds of bodily care, cuddling, and "conversing" face to face. Secure attachment (Bowlby, 1988) and other essential learning take place during the repeated interactions of nurturing routines. Diapering, bathing, dressing, and feeding are important times for the care not just of the infant's body, but also of his mind. If the adult is calm and focused on trying to understand what the infant is feeling and experiencing, the adult can respectfully draw the infant's attention to the task at hand in such a way that he finds pleasure in sharing attention to the task (Tardos & Appell, 1992). This sets up a willingness on the part of the infant to cooperate with significant adults—an important habit for success later on, in school.

Savannah (4 months) has just awakened and is lying in her crib cooing at the ring toy she is playing with. She bangs it against the bars of the crib and notices the sound it makes. She tries it again and hears a similar sound. Savannah is noticing that when she bangs harder, the sound is louder and so is the pressure of the toy on the edge of her hand. She is paying attention to her actions and reactions, putting cause and effect together, and generally practicing the integration of her senses. Now her mother, Marie, arrives into her field of view and, smiling, says, "Hi! You woke up. I think you are ready for a diaper change," and holds out her hands indicating that she will pick Savannah up. Savannah smiles at her mother, but continues banging the toy and kicking her legs—not quite ready to give up her play. Her mother says, "You like that toy; you are having fun banging it" and waits a moment, until her daughter seems to have finished her experiments. Then she removes the toy from the baby's hand, gently, and says, "I will give you your ring back after we change your diaper. Now I will pick you up." Noting that the baby has adjusted her body in preparation to be picked up, her mother slides her hands under Savannah's back and lifts her slowly, taking care not to allow her head to flop or her spine to wobble. Marie carries her to the changing table and takes equal care lowering Savannah slowly onto the new surface. (Slow movement by Marie allows Savannah's bodily integrity to remain intact in order for her attention to stay with Marie and smoothly transition to the task at hand.) Marie speaks to Savannah about the diaper change, and does not try to distract her or rush through it just to get it finished. She asks Savannah to participate in the process, either just with her attention or even, increasingly, with cooperative actions. Touching the diaper lightly, Marie says, "I need to open the diaper. Can you lower your legs, please?" Then Marie waits until Savannah does so, either by design or accident, and only then untapes the diaper. (The waiting is just as important as the words and actions; the waiting is what truly communicates respect. Accommodating the infant's slow reaction time is the key to making room for her active participation and

full presence in the moment.) Savannah notices the bracelet
Marie is wearing and, grasping it, brings it to her mouth.
Because Marie is interested in allowing Savannah to attend to
her interests, she lets her mouth the smooth, cool silver for a
moment, until Savannah looks at her face. Having regained her
daughter's attention, Marie returns to the diapering process.
When the diaper change is over, Marie carries Savannah to her
play space, slowly puts her down—again, making sure the transi-
tion is smooth so that Savannah does not startle when put
down—and says, "I'll be back in a minute to watch you play. I
need to wash my hands and get a drink of water first."

Taking the toy away from the baby before going to the changing table is a signal that Marie wants Savannah's undivided attention. It is particularly important to involve infants and toddlers in the intimacies of bodily care. RIE practitioners do not want them to tune out to their own sensations while they are being touched. We want them to tune in. By tuning in, they learn that their bodies are their business, which will set them up for a lifetime of self-respect. By tuning in, babies learn that they have an effect on how interactions go. Paradoxically, from being allowed to let their attention wander to other things during the task, they learn that others are willing to accommodate their wishes, to a point, which lessens frustration and resistance. The key is to leave behind most distractions— such as toys, random singing, or chitchat—that have nothing to do with the diaper change so that attention will be mutually focused on the task in a pleasant, unhurried way. Yes, the baby will find things to take her attention away from the task anyway, but why make it easier to get distracted by bringing toys to the care situation? Care routines are about the relationship. There is plenty of time for objects during playtime. Multitasking is the opposite of paying attention deeply.

In addition to this attention-with-a-partner, it is beneficial for even very young babies to spend some of their quiet–alert time lying unrestrained on a firm mattress or blanket in a safe, peaceful, quiet place so that they can tune into their own bodies. With hunger and the need for rest satisfied, a baby is ready to pay attention to his other internal and external experiences. With his attention focused on himself, he might be thinking the following thoughts: "Where am I? What is around me? What is that motion I am sensing?" ("Oh, it's my leg moving!") "What's this I'm feeling with my fingers by my side?" ("The blanket? Oh, soft!") "What's that pressure?" ("Ah . . . gas gurgle.") This is a chance for a baby to relax into himself. If a baby is peacefully looking at his hands, turning them one way and another, looking at the empty space between his fingers, opening and closing them, this is important baby work. Often, though, when infants are engaged in such a self-chosen activity, an adult will not notice the interest with which the baby is attending and come over and start talking to him or shaking a rattle in his face.

Sometimes adults interrupt with a narrative of what the baby is doing, thinking it is time for a vocabulary lesson. However, this may also seriously disrupt her thoughts. Imagine you are working and someone is standing behind you giving a running commentary: "Oh, I see you are working on your book. You are typing fast! Your fingers are just flying! You are using lots and lots of words. What a good job!" This would be annoying and distracting, yes? It would be absurd; but well-meaning people do that to infants and toddlers all the time. Of course, there are times adults must interrupt for a good reason, but interrupting when there is not a good reason teaches infants that getting too interested in something is not allowed. Sometimes a random interruption could be a sign that the adult is not paying attention to the child or has become bored. Of course, when the baby looks at the adult to share her pleasure or discomfort, then is the time to speak appropriate words. Not everyone is cut out to be a professional baby watcher (like my RIE companions and me), but learning to appreciate how the infant uses her attention makes interrupting more obvious. Another benefit of periods of independent play is that they allow a lone caregiver the opportunity to attend to laundry, other children, or phone calls for a little while. In a safe environment, a baby can play freely without being watched constantly. (This is information that needs to be conveyed judiciously. If a person's judgment of what is safe is suspect, better to encourage more watchfulness.)

It is important for the adult always to tell even the tiniest baby when one is going to walk away, and when one will be back. This way, the baby can learn to trust that if you have not said you were leaving, then you are there within sight. This extra effort to communicate your whereabouts with the baby may feel silly at first, while the baby is very young and seems not to care. It pays huge dividends later, though, when separation anxiety becomes a factor, as she can remain confident in her sense of knowing what is going on—even if she does not like the fact that you have walked away. A baby who is not anxious from not knowing her caregiver's whereabouts can attend to other interesting elements in the environment, demonstrating basic trust. Certainly babies whose significant adults do not practice this way of showing respect can be securely attached, but babies whose adults do warn before walking away may be just a little more secure. Is it possible to be too securely attached? One further note on this point: Even if you are not the parent or primary carer, it pays to let babies know if you will be walking away from them, where you are going, and when you will be back. Having people popping into and out of one's presence unexpectedly is disconcerting and does not build security. Even though, as just their RIE facilitator, I am not an essential person to the babies and toddlers in my classes, I can see clearly that their peaceful attention is disrupted if I walk out of the room without warning, even though all of their parents are there. If this is the case, how much more disturbing for a child whose primary caregiver keeps disappearing and reappearing without explanation?

An infant peacefully playing on a blanket in front of the window is using his attention to notice many things, and even to control some of them.

> *Five-month-old Diego gazes up to see the green leaves swaying against the blue sky outside the window of his child care room. A moment later, he feels a cooling on his skin from the breeze that wafts through the window. This excites him to squeeze his hand, in which he finds a piece of stiff cotton. He raises his fist, clutching the napkin, and suddenly the light changes. He begins to experiment with light and shadow, raising and lowering his arm so the cloth passes between his eyes and the window. After several passes, he drops the napkin behind his head and in reaching for it begins to stretch and struggle. His desire for the object motivates him to master his movements, to try to reach the cloth. Diego begins the process of trying to turn over, struggling until he is too frustrated to continue. When he cries, his caregiver comes over to see what he needs. He has turned partway over, but is stuck on his arm. His caregiver watches for a moment to see if he can solve his problem by himself, but finally says, "Oh, Diego, I think you are feeling stuck. I will help you turn back over," and she gently returns him to his back. She stays with him for a few moments, resetting some toys around him that he will be able to reach, then tells him it is time for her to change Sam's diaper. He resumes his play, knowing he will have more time with her later because she is sensitively attuned to his need for interaction (co-regulation) as well as his need for quiet play on his own (auto-regulation). A healthy balance of these two ways of maintaining homeostasis is what self-regulation is about* (Schore, 1994).

Of course, many factors play a part in helping babies learn to concentrate, but a very important one is maintaining a sensory environment that invites babies to seek engagement rather than screen out an overabundance of stimulation. If during this productive playtime, a radio or TV in the background distracted him every few seconds, or an adult interrupted by randomly offering a toy, he might not develop the habit of continuously paying attention to the problem before him. He would

not get the self-reinforcing feedback that concentration pays off.
He might develop the habit of
giving up without trying.

Caregivers know that infants
and toddlers are attracted to novelty in the environment, but if
reinforce this too much, they
undermine the beneficial effects of
a little healthy boredom. Babies
and children who are offered too
much—too many new toys or con-
stant entertainment—do not have a chance to learn to keep themselves
interested by creatively using and combining the same-old same-old toys.
I am reminded of Everett, the active toddler in my RIE group who had
already exploited all of the dumping and filling possibilities offered by the
square 3-gallon water jug and basket of hair curlers that were always in
the playroom. The same toys and equipment are there every week, and
one week he changed his approach. Everett began pushing the jug all
around the carpeted floor, figuring out what to do when objects or the
other babies got in his way. He did some interesting problem solving with
that pesky first law of physics (two bodies cannot occupy the same space
at the same time). Within another couple of weeks, he began pushing the
jug up and down the low slide and then later up and over the archlike
stair climber, as I wrote of in chapter 6. With the same objects, over time,
he used creativity to make them into different activities. In a nutshell:
Less is—or becomes—more.

Overall, the prescription offered by the RIE approach in the modern
world for academic, functional, and relational success is not some new
method of child rearing or product, but rather the willingness of adults
to see that each child has sufficient access to trusted attachment figures
(a) who are fully present during caregiving moments, (b) who provide the
setting and time for autonomous exploration (play), and (c) who take the
trouble to screen out children's exposure to harmful or extraneous stimuli
as best they can. These three foundational necessities allow infants and
toddlers to focus their attention on what is truly important, which in early
childhood is the satisfaction of relationships with attuned adults, the joy
of discovery, play with peers, and the rewards of creative problem solving
(Hammond, 2004). By offering these gifts to infants and toddlers, adults
will make their own involvement more peaceful and rewarding, and
maybe, as Magda Gerber always said, contribute to a more respectful
world (1986).

References

Bowlby, J. (1988). *A secure base.* New York: Basic Books.

Colombo, J., & Cheatham, C. L. (2006). The emergence and basis of endogenous attention in infancy and early childhood: Vol. 34. *Advances in child development and behavior.* London: Academic Press/Elsevier.

Gerber, M. (Ed.). (1979). *The RIE manual for parents and professionals.* Los Angeles: Resources for Infant Educarers.

Gerber, M. (1986). *Seeing infants with new eyes* [DVD]. Los Angeles: Resources for Infant Educarers.

Gerber, M. (2002). *Dear parent: Caring for infants with respect* (expanded edition). Los Angeles: Resources for Infant Educarers.

Hammond, R.A. (2004). Paying attention. *Educaring, 24(1-2)*, p.1–8.

Oxford illustrated dictionary. (1998). New York: Oxford University Press.

Pawl, J. (2006). Being held in another's mind. In R. J. Lally, P. Mangione, & D. Greenwald (Eds.), *Concepts for care* (pp. 1–6). San Francisco: WestEd.

Roche, M. A. (Ed.). (1994). Emmi Pikler 1902–1984 [Special issue]. *Sensory Awareness Foundation Bulletin, 14.*

Schore, A. N. (1994). *Affect regulation and the repair of the self.* Hillsdale, NJ: Erlbaum.

Schore, A. N. (2003). *Affect regulation and the origin of the self.* New York: W.W. Norton & Co.

Tardos, A., & Appell, G. (1992). *Paying attention to each other: Infant and adult during the bath* [DVD]. Budapest, Hungary: The Pikler Institute.

Williamson, G., & Anzalone, M. (2001). *Sensory integration and self-regulation in infants and toddlers.* Washington, DC: ZERO TO THREE.

Ruth Anne Hammond, MA, is a specialist in infant–toddler development and caregiving. A working mother and professional, she has led the Pacific Oaks Infant/Toddler-Parent Program in Pasadena, California, since 1996. Trained by Resources for Infant Educarers (RIE) founder Magda Gerber, Hammond is a mentor/teacher Associate and president of the Board of Directors of RIE, a nonprofit world-wide membership organization, dedicated to improving the quality of infant care and education through teaching, supporting, and mentoring parents and caregivers. Hammond also teaches infancy courses at Pacific Oaks College, and studies affective neuroscience with Allan N. Schore, PhD, of the UCLA David Geffen School of Medicine. She and her husband live in Los Angeles and have a son and a daughter.